Weekly Lesson Tests
Copying Masters

Grade 1

Harcourt School Publishers

www.harcourtschool.com

Printed in the United States of America

ISBN 10 0-15-351713-1   ISBN 13 978-0-15-351713-6

2 3 4 5 6 7 8 9 10   862   16 15 14 13 12 11 10 09 08 07

Contents

© Harcourt • Grade 1

Contents

Contents

Selection Comprehension

▶ **Fill in the circle next to the correct answer.**

1. What is this story about?

○ tap dancing

○ tapping a drum

○ singing songs

2. Where are the children?

○ at an art class

○ at a birthday party

○ at a dance

3. How do the children learn to tap?

○ They watch TV.

○ They help each other

○ They look at pictures.

4. How do the children feel when they tap?

○ happy

○ sleepy

○ bored

Name _____

▶ **Draw or write an answer to the question.**

5. What is something else that can tap?

[ ]

_____

- -

_____

_____

- -

_____

_____

- -

_____

Name _____

Phonics/Spelling: Short Vowel /a/a

▶ **Fill in the circle under the word that names
each picture.**

1.

man   me   my
○   ○   ○

2.

out   can   come
○   ○   ○

3.

map   mom   and
○   ○   ○

4.

dog   come   cat
○   ○   ○

Phonics/Spelling: Short Vowel /a/a   7

Name _____

Phonics/Spelling: Inflections -s

▶ **Fill in the circle under the word that completes each sentence.**

5.

cat   cats   catz

○   ○   ○

6.

maps   map   mats

○   ○   ○

7.

cans   cap   caps

○   ○   ○

8.

vans   tag   van

○   ○   ○

Phonics/Spelling: Inflections -s   8   **TOTAL SCORE:** _____ /8

High-Frequency Words

▶ **Write a word from the box to complete each sentence.**

help	let's	now

_____
- - - - - - - - - - - - - - - - - -

1. _____ walk the dog.

_____
- - - - - - - - - - - - - - - - - -

2. They _____ look
for the ball.

_____
- - - - - - - - - - - - - - - - - -

3. She will eat _____.

TOTAL SCORE: _____ /3

Focus Skill: Make Predictions

▶ **Look at the pictures. Fill in the circle under
the sentence that tells what happens next.**

1. Sara rides in the car.   Sara pats the dog.

2. The girls go home.   The girls play ball.

Name _____

3.   Sam helps.   Sam eats.

         ◯   ◯

4.   The dog runs.   The dog naps.

         ◯   ◯

Focus Skill: Make Predictions   11   **TOTAL SCORE:** _____ /4

Name _____

Robust Vocabulary

▶ **Fill in the circle next to the correct answer.**

I. If you are <u>bothered</u> by a bee, what might you do?

　○ draw a picture of it

　○ make a buzzing noise

　○ run away from it

2. If you see a sign at a <u>distance</u>, how close are you to it?

　○ near it

　○ far from it

　○ next to it

3. Which one could you <u>form</u> best with clay?

　○ your lunch

　○ a bowl

　○ water

4. If you <u>instruct</u> someone, what might you do?

○ teach

○ listen

○ play

5. If you <u>perform</u> in a show, what might you do?

○ walk to school

○ talk to a friend

○ play the piano

6. If you are <u>supportive</u> of your friends, how do you feel?

○ you are happy

○ you are bored

○ you believe in them

© Harcourt • Grade 1

Grammar: Sentences

▶ **Fill in the circle under each sentence that is written correctly.**

I.   The cat.   I see the map.

          ○   ○

2.   He ran fast.   good dogs

          ○   ○

3.   I can see the man.   Is red.

          ○   ○

4.   a little mat   The hat is red.

          ○   ○

TOTAL SCORE: _____ /4

Name _____

Selection Comprehension

▶ **Fill in the circle next to the correct answer.**

1. Where are the friends probably going?

   ○ to a movie

   ○ on a picnic

   ○ to a book store

2. Why can't the van go?

   ○ It is too full.

   ○ It is out of gas.

   ○ It has no wheels.

3. What happens at the end of the story?

   ○ Jan brings a wagon.

   ○ Jan takes her friends home.

   ○ Jan brings a big van.

4. Why could this story never happen?

   ○ Animals do not eat food.

   ○ Animals do not have vans.

   ○ Animals do not sit together.

Name _____

▶ **Draw or write an answer to the question.**

5. What helps the van go?

```




```

_____

- - - - - - - - - - - - - - - - - - - -

_____

_____

- - - - - - - - - - - - - - - - - - - -

_____

_____

- - - - - - - - - - - - - - - - - - - -

_____

Selection Comprehension
"The Van"

16

TOTAL SCORE: _____ /4 + _____ /2

© Harcourt • Grade 1

Phonics/Spelling: Short Vowel /a/a

▶ **Fill in the circle under the word that names each picture.**

1.

she	sad	see
○	○	○

2.

nap	now	sat
○	○	○

3.

bam	bat	boy
○	○	○

4.

lap	mat	bag
○	○	○

Phonics/Spelling: Short Vowel /a/a   **17**   TOTAL SCORE: _____ /4

Name _____

High-Frequency Words

▶ **Write a word from the box to complete each sentence.**

in	no	too

1. The jam is _____ the bag.

_____

_____

2. She can play _____.

_____

_____

3. _____, do not jump on the bed.

High-Frequency Words

18

TOTAL SCORE: _____ /3

Name _____

Focus Skill: Make Predictions

▶ **Look at the pictures. Fill in the circle under the sentence that tells what happens next.**

1.   The cat eats.

The cat naps.

2.   Mark plays with a toy.

Mark helps his mom.

Focus Skill: Make Predictions

19

© Harcourt • Grade 1

3. Ann gets a hat.   Ann looks at her mother.

4. Ben comes home.   Ben gets in the van.

Focus Skill: Make Predictions

TOTAL SCORE: _____ /4

Name _____

Robust Vocabulary

▶ **Fill in the circle next to the correct answer.**

1. Which thing could be <u>nearby</u>?

   ○ a cloud

   ○ the top of a very tall building

   ○ a desk

2. Which one might give you a <u>fright</u>?

   ○ packing your lunch

   ○ hearing loud thunder

   ○ putting away your toys

3. Where would Pam go to study if she wanted
   to <u>escape</u> from her noisy house?

   ○ the movies

   ○ the library

   ○ the park

4. What might happen if you <u>cram</u> too many things into your suitcase?

○ The suitcase might be heavy.

○ The suitcase might change color.

○ The suitcase might get lost.

5. If you have a <u>solution</u> to a problem, what do you have?

○ a story

○ the answer

○ a wish

6. If you have a <u>strategy</u>, what do you have?

○ a plan

○ a game

○ a team

TOTAL SCORE: _____ /6

Grammar: Word Order

▶ **Fill in the circle under the sentence where the words make sense.**

1. The cat likes to play.   Likes to play the cat.
            ○   ○

2. Down here dad sat.   Dad sat down here.
            ○   ○

3. Go to the zoo I like to.   I like to go to the zoo.
            ○   ○

4. Pat wants that toy car.   That toy car Pat wants.
            ○   ○

TOTAL SCORE: _____ /4

Name _____

Selection Comprehension

▶ **Fill in the circle next to the correct answer.**

1. What does a big rig do?

   ○ It carries things.

   ○ It makes things.

   ○ It fixes things.

2. Which one is smaller than a big rig?

   ○ a tall building

   ○ a jet plane

   ○ a car

3. What can you tell about Dad?

   ○ He likes to fly.

   ○ He likes to drive.

   ○ He likes to walk.

4. How does the girl feel about Dad's job?

   ○ sorry

   ○ proud

   ○ puzzled

▶ **Draw or write an answer to the question.**

5. What is one thing a big rig might carry?

Phonics/Spelling: Short Vowel /i/ i

▶ **Fill in the circle under the word that names each picture.**

1.

pin	pan	pat
○	○	○

2.

pill	pat	pig
○	○	○

3.

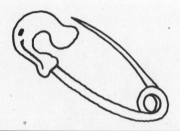

lap	list	lid
○	○	○

4.

bib	big	bat
○	○	○

TOTAL SCORE: _____ /4

Phonics/Spelling: Contractions 's

▶ **Fill in the circle under the words that name the underlined contraction.**

I. <u>He's</u> sad.

He is   He goes   He us
○   ○   ○

_____

2. <u>It's</u> my cat.

It us   It was   It is
○   ○   ○

_____

3. <u>She's</u> in the car.

She is   She us   She says
○   ○   ○

_____

4. <u>Here's</u> the
red cap.

Here was   Here is   Here goes
○   ○   ○

TOTAL SCORE: _____ /4

Name _____

High-Frequency Words

▶ **Write a word from the box to complete each sentence.**

> get   hold   home   so   soon

1. Jeff is at _____ .

2. I _____ the pot.

3. That cat is _____ big!

_____

----

4. I can _____ the jam.

_____

----

5. I will get out of bed _____.

Name _____

Focus Skill: Classify/Categorize

▶ **Fill in the circle under the picture that answers each question.**

1. Which picture shows something that belongs in the category "animals"?

○   ○

2. Which picture shows something that belongs in the category "plants"?

○   ○

Focus Skill: Classify/Categorize   30

3. Which picture shows something that belongs in the category "ways to play"?

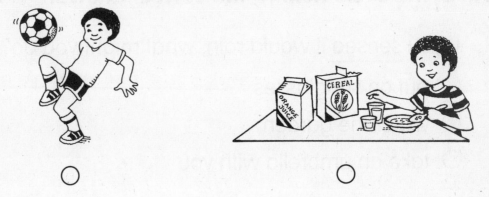

○   ○

4. Which picture shows something that belongs in the category "food"?

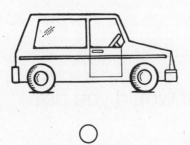   

○   ○

Focus Skill: Classify/Categorize   31   TOTAL SCORE: _____ /6

Name _____

Robust Vocabulary

▶ **Fill in the circle next to the correct answer.**

1. If you <u>sensed</u> it would rain, what might you do?

   ○ put on sunglasses

   ○ water the garden

   ○ take an umbrella with you

2. If you were <u>especially</u> happy, how might you feel?

   ○ very happy

   ○ not happy

   ○ a little happy

3. If you <u>memorize</u> a poem, what would you do?

   ○ write it

   ○ make it into a song

   ○ remember all the words

Name _____

4. Which one would fit into the box with the smallest <u>capacity</u>?

○ a stove

○ a shoe

○ a ring

5. When might you be <u>proud</u> of yourself?

○ after doing poorly on a test

○ after finding a home for a kitten

○ after losing your new jacket

6. Which one would someone use to <u>haul</u> furniture?

○ car

○ truck

○ bicycle

Robust Vocabulary

33

TOTAL SCORE: _____ /6

© Harcourt • Grade 1

Grammar: Naming parts of sentences

▶ **Underline the naming part of each sentence.**

1. Dan will have milk.

_____

2. I like to look at birds.

_____

3. The bear runs up the hill.

_____

4. We sit in the car.

TOTAL SCORE: _____ /4

Teacher Read-Aloud

Name _____

Weekly
Lesson Test
. . . .
.Lesson 4

Selection Comprehension

▶ **Fill in the circle next to the correct answer.**

1. Where does Rick live?

○ on a ranch

○ near a lake

○ in a big city

---

2. Why did Rick sleep too long?

○ He was sick.

○ His clock broke.

○ He stayed up late.

---

3. Why do the animals put a gift on Rick's table?

○ to surprise him

○ to trick him

○ to trap him

---

4. Why could this story never happen?

○ Roosters do not crow.

○ Roosters do not sleep.

○ Roosters do not use clocks.

▶ **Draw or write an answer to the question.**

5. What was the gift the animals gave Rick?

```
┌─────────────────────────────────────────────┐
│                                             │
│                                             │
│                                             │
│                                             │
│                                             │
│                                             │
│                                             │
│                                             │
│                                             │
└─────────────────────────────────────────────┘
```

_____

- -

_____

- -

_____

- -

Name _____

Phonics/Spelling: Digraph /k/ck

▶ **Fill in the circle under the picture that contains the sound *ck*.**

1. ck

    ◯   ◯   ◯

2. ck

    ◯   ◯   ◯

3. ck

    ◯   ◯   ◯

4. ck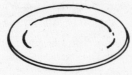

    ◯   ◯   ◯

TOTAL SCORE: _____ /4

High-Frequency Words

▶ **Write a word from the box to complete each sentence.**

| late   oh   yes |

1. _____, Ann can add.

2. I am _____.

3. _____ no! The cat is sick.

Name _____

Focus Skill: Story Elements (Beginning, Middle, End)

▶ **Read the story. Fill in the circle under the picture that is the answer to each question.**

Sam went into the room. It was the first day in his new class. He did not know anyone.

Soon, it was time to eat. The children walked to a big room. Sam sat alone. He liked his old class better.

A girl came to sit next to him. "I am Liz. It is nice to meet you."

"Yes," said Sam. "I am glad to meet you, too."

Sam had made a new friend.

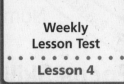

1. Which picture tells what happens at the
beginning of this story?

○   ○   ○

2. Which picture tells what happens in the middle
of this story?

○   ○   ○

3. Which picture tells what happens at the ending
of this story?

○   ○   ○

**Focus Skill: Story Elements
(Beginning, Middle, End)**

40

TOTAL SCORE: _____ /3

Name _____

Robust Vocabulary

▶ **Fill in the circle next to the correct answer.**

I. If you <u>pouted</u>, how might you feel?

   ○ very happy

   ○ tired

   ○ not happy

2. If you <u>ambled</u> down the street, what did you do?

   ○ hopped

   ○ ran quickly

   ○ walked slowly

3. If you acted <u>politely</u>, what did you do?

   ○ showed good manners

   ○ spoke loudly

   ○ fell asleep too soon

4. Which one might be <u>routine</u> for you in the morning?

○ bathing a dog

○ brushing your teeth

○ eating a big dinner

---

5. If you were <u>considerate</u> of others, what would you do?

○ think about their feelings

○ talk out of turn

○ hurt the feelings of others

---

6. Which one might be <u>unexpected</u>?

○ having a surprise party

○ talking with a friend

○ reading a good book

Grammar: Telling Parts of Sentences

▶ **Fill in the circle next to the telling part of each sentence.**

1. The pigs roll in the mud.

   ○ The pigs

   ○ roll in the mud

   ○ the mud

2. Jack looks at the teacher.

   ○ Jack

   ○ teacher

   ○ looks at the teacher

3. The tan cat licks my hand.

   ○ licks my hand

   ○ The tan cat

   ○ my hand

TOTAL SCORE: _____ /3

Selection Comprehension

▶ **Fill in the circle next to the correct answer.**

1. What does Mom want to do?

   ○ sell something

   ○ plant something

   ○ make something

2. Why does Bob dig the hole?

   ○ He is hot.

   ○ He wants to plant the tree.

   ○ He likes to dig.

3. Why doesn't the tree fit at first?

   ○ The hole is too deep.

   ○ The tree is too big.

   ○ The hole needs to be bigger.

4. Why does Bob kick and kick?

   ○ to scratch his feet

   ○ to fill the hole

   ○ to play a game

Name _____

▶ **Draw or write an answer to the question.**

5. What happens at the end of the story?

[box for drawing]

_____
- -
_____
_____
- -
_____
_____
- -
_____

Selection Comprehension
"Dot and Bob"

TOTAL SCORE: _____ /4 + _____ /2

Name _____

Phonics/Spelling: Short Vowel /o/o

▶ **Fill in the circle under the word that names each picture.**

1.

lamp	lid	lock
○	○	○

2.

hop	hip	hold
○	○	○

3.

fix	fan	fox
○	○	○

4.

dad	dot	dig
○	○	○

TOTAL SCORE: _____ /4

Phonics/Spelling: Inflections *-ed, -ing*

▶ **Fill in the circle beside the word that best completes each sentence.**

I. I like _____ with the girl next door.

○ playing

○ plays

○ played

2. Mark _____ the tub with water.

○ filling

○ filled

○ fill

3. We _____ to school.

○ walking

○ walked

○ walks

4. Mom is _____ the car door.

○ locking

○ locked

○ lock

TOTAL SCORE: _____ /4

Name _____

High-Frequency Words

▶ **Write a word from the box to complete each
sentence.**

find	much	thank

1. That is too _____ .

_____

2. _____ you for the
hat.

_____

3. I cannot _____ my
dog.

High-Frequency Words   48   TOTAL SCORE: _____ /3

Name _____

Focus Skill: Story Elements (Characters)

▶ **Read each sentence. Fill in the circle under the picture that shows the character in each sentence.**

1. Hank locked the box.

○   ○

2. Todd sank in the sand.

○   ○

3. Jan kicked the ball.

○   ○

Focus Skill: Story Elements (Characters)   **49**

4. Pam took a nap.

○   ○

5. They sat on a rock.

○   ○

6. The ducks are in the pond.

   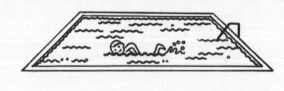

○   ○

Focus Skill: Story Elements (Characters)   50   TOTAL SCORE: _____ /6

Robust Vocabulary

▶ **Fill in the circle next to the correct answer.**

I. Which might have a <u>horrible</u> smell?

○ old garbage

○ an orange

○ a flower

2. If you are <u>invigorated</u>, how do you feel?

○ tired and bored

○ ready to cry

○ full of energy

3. If you <u>presented</u> someone with a gift, what did you do?

○ gave it to them

○ read it to them

○ sold it to them

4. If it is a <u>sweltering</u> day, what might you do?

   ○ drink something cold

   ○ eat some hot soup

   ○ wear a jacket

5. For which one might you need to ask for <u>aid</u>?

   ○ moving a chair

   ○ eating an apple

   ○ talking to a friend

6. If you are <u>persistent</u> in learning to play the piano, what might you do?

   ○ play soccer after school

   ○ practice every day

   ○ read a book about cats

Grammar: Telling Sentences

▶ **Fill in the circle beside each telling sentence.**

I. Which one is a telling sentence?

  ○ She can hop.

  ○ She can hop

  ○ she can hop

2. Which one is a telling sentence?

  ○ mom has the mop

  ○ Mom has the mop.

  ○ mom has the mop.

3. Which one is a telling sentence?

  ○ Her backpack is red.

  ○ Her backpack is red

  ○ her backpack is red.

4. Which one is a telling sentence?

  ○ that book is his

  ○ That book is his

  ○ That book is his.

Selection Comprehension

▶ **Fill in the circle next to the correct answer.**

1. What is the story about?

○ how to use a map

○ how to travel to a town

○ how to climb a hill.

2. What do ALL the children like?

○ hills

○ maps

○ tall buildings

3. What do the children do at the END?

○ make a map

○ visit a town hall

○ ride a fire truck

4. What does this story have?

○ animals that talk

○ words that sound alike

○ things you see in real life

▶ **Draw or write an answer to the question.**

5. What is something you can find on a map?

_____

- -

_____

- -

_____

- -

_____

Name _____

Contractions *n't*

▶ **Fill in the circle next to the words that name the underlined contraction in each sentence.**

1. I <u>haven't</u> locked the box.

   ○ have not

   ○ has not

   ○ how not

2. That <u>isn't</u> my cat.

   ○ is not

   ○ are not

   ○ has not

3. Sal <u>didn't</u> see the pig.

   ○ do not

   ○ did not

   ○ does not

4. Bill and Bob <u>aren't</u> going to the pond.

   ○ am not

   ○ act not

   ○ are not

TOTAL SCORE: _____ /4

High-Frequency Words

▶ **Write a word from the box to complete
each sentence.**

| how | make | of | some |

_____

----

1. Pam will _____ a gift for Ross.

_____

----

2. This is _____ I hit the ball.

_____

----

3. All _____ the girls are here.

_____

----

4. Kim lost _____ of her socks.

TOTAL SCORE: _____ /4

Name _____

Focus Skill: Classify/Categorize

▶ **Look at the three pictures. Fill in the circle under the picture that does not belong.**

I.

   ○   ○   ○

2.

   ○   ○   ○

3.

   ○   ○   ○

4.

   ○   ○   ○

Name _____

▶ **Fill in the circle that best names the category for the three pictures shown.**

5.

- ○ things to eat
- ○ things to wear
- ○ things to drink

6.

- ○ places to sleep
- ○ bodies of water
- ○ kinds of weather

7.

- ○ kinds of fish
- ○ names of animals
- ○ ways to travel

Focus Skill: Classify/Categorize   59   TOTAL SCORE: _____ /7

© Harcourt • Grade 1

Name _____

Robust Vocabulary

▶ **Fill in the circle next to the correct answer.**

1. Which one might help you <u>locate</u> your school?

   ○ an apple

   ○ a cup

   ○ a map

2. Which one is a <u>symbol</u> of our country?

   ○ a child

   ○ a flag

   ○ a car

3. Which one might cause a <u>commotion</u>?

   ○ a barking dog

   ○ a sleeping child

   ○ a falling leaf

4. If you <u>muffle</u> a sound, what do you do?

   ○ make it louder

   ○ make it quieter

   ○ keep it the same

5. Which one helps you <u>search</u> for something in the dark?

  ○ a lamp

  ○ a sock

  ○ a mop

---

6. Why might a glass be <u>overflowing</u>?

  ○ Someone poured the right amount.

  ○ Someone poured too little.

  ○ Someone poured too much.

TOTAL SCORE: _____ /6

Grammar: Questions

▶ **Fill in the circle next to each correct answer.**

1. Which one is a question?

○ Jill hit the ball.

○ Did Jill hit the ball?

○ Jill did hit the ball.

---

2. Which one is a question?

○ Where is my cap?

○ She has my cap.

○ My cap is not here.

---

3. Which one is a question?

○ Six ducks swim in the pond.

○ Do the ducks swim in the pond?

○ Six ducks are in the pond.

---

4. Which one is a question?

○ Ask Mom for Tom's hat.

○ Mom has Tom's hat.

○ Where is Tom's hat?

TOTAL SCORE: _____ /4

Selection Comprehension

▶ **Fill in the circle next to the correct answer.**

1. At first, why won't the animals eat Red Hen's food?

○ They are tired of the food.

○ The food is burned.

○ The food is cold.

---

2. What do Cat, Fox, Pig, and Red Hen ALL want to do?

○ clean

○ bake

○ eat

---

3. What happens at the END?

○ Red Hen asks who wants to eat.

○ Ants help pick up the mess.

○ The animals help make food.

---

4. The next time Red Hen has food, who will
she ask to eat with her?

○ Fox

○ Ant

○ Pig

▶ **Draw or write an answer to the question.**

5. Who makes a big mess in the story?

_____
- -
_____
_____
- -
_____
_____
- -
_____

Name _____

Phonics/Spelling: Short Vowel /e/e

▶ **Fill in the circle under the word that names each picture.**

1.

tack	tint	tent
○	○	○

2.

dock	desk	disk
○	○	○

3.

leg	lid	log
○	○	○

4.

nick	nest	nod
○	○	○

TOTAL SCORE: _____ /4

Phonics/Spelling: Initial Blends with *l*

▶ Fill in the circle under the word that begins
with the letters shown.

1. cl

○   ○   ○

2. bl

 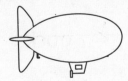

○   ○   ○

3. pl

○   ○   ○

4. gl

  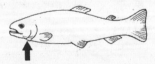

○   ○   ○

TOTAL SCORE: _____ /4

Name _____

High-Frequency Words

▶ **Write a word from the box to complete each sentence.**

day	eat	first	said	time	was

1. Sal _____ going to bed.

_____

2. What _____ will we go to camp?

_____

3. We will _____ the hot dogs.

_____

4. The king _____ that he wanted a pet.

5. Is it _____ for us to go
fishing?

6. This is the _____ time I will see
a sunset.

Name _____

Focus Skill: Compare and Contrast

▶ **Fill in the answer circles under the two pictures that are alike.**

1.

○   ○   ○

2.

○   ○   ○

Focus Skill: Compare and Contrast   69

© Harcourt • Grade 1

▶ **Fill in the answer circle under the picture that is different from the other pictures.**

3.

  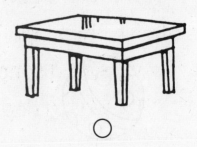

○   ○   ○

4.

○   ○   ○

Focus Skill: Compare and Contrast

TOTAL SCORE: _____ /4

Robust Vocabulary

▶ **Fill in the circle next to the correct answer.**

1. If you are part of a <u>chorus</u>, what might you do?
   - ○ bat a ball
   - ○ sing a song
   - ○ walk a dog

2. Which one has an unpleasant <u>odor</u>?
   - ○ a skunk
   - ○ a rose
   - ○ a bakery

3. If you <u>shoved</u> a chair, what did you do?
   - ○ pushed hard against it
   - ○ turned it upside down
   - ○ fell asleep on it

4. If you <u>assemble</u> a sandwich, which one do you need?
   - ○ bread
   - ○ apple
   - ○ puppy

5. Which one is something you <u>consume</u>?

   ○ a rock

   ○ some trees

   ○ ice cream

6. Which one might make you <u>enthusiastic</u>?

   ○ missing a friend's visit

   ○ winning a big game

   ○ losing something important

Name _____

Grammar: Exclamations

▶ **Fill in the circle next to each exclamation.**

1. Which one is an exclamation?
   ○ Maria hit the ball.
   ○ Maria hit it far!
   ○ Did Maria hit the ball?

2. Which one is an exclamation?
   ○ What a big mess!
   ○ Did you spill the milk?
   ○ I saw Dan spill the milk.

3. Which one is an exclamation?
   ○ Did you see that little dog?
   ○ The black dog is little.
   ○ That black dog is so little!

4. Which one is an exclamation?
   ○ Jess lost his raft.
   ○ Is the raft lost?
   ○ Oh, no! Jess lost his raft!

Grammar: Exclamations   73   TOTAL SCORE: _____ /4

Weekly
Lesson Test
· · · · · · · · · · · ·
Lesson 8

Selection Comprehension

▶ **Fill in the circle next to the correct answer.**

1. Where does the story take place?

○ at Beth's house

○ at a plant store

○ at school

___

2. What does Beth want?

○ a new job

○ a new book

○ a new friend

___

3. What happens to Beth's plant?

○ It stays the same.

○ It gets too dry.

○ It grows.

___

4. How are all the children the SAME?

○ All feed a pet.

○ All have a job.

○ All hold a flag.

Name _____

▶ **Draw or write an answer to the question.**

5. What makes Beth like her job at the end of the story?

Name _____

Phonics/Spelling: Digraph /th/*th*

▶ Fill in the circle under the picture that contains the sound *th*.

1. th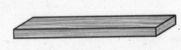

   ○   ○   ○

2. th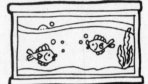

   ○   ○   ○

3. th

   ○   ○   ○

4. th

   ○   ○   ○

TOTAL SCORE: _____ /4

Phonics/Spelling: Initial Blends with *s*

▶ **Fill in the circle under the word that begins with the letters shown.**

1. sl

○   ○   ○

2. sw

○   ○   ○

3. sl

○   ○   ○

4. sn

○   ○   ○

TOTAL SCORE: _____ /4

High-Frequency Words

▶ **Write a word from the box to complete each sentence.**

| water   her   Mr.   don't   says   new   line |

_____
- -
1. I _____ have a pencil.

_____
- -
2. Mrs. Smith's pen is on _____ desk.

_____
- -
3. We got in a _____ to go to art class.

_____
- -
4. _____ Gill went to the pond.

Name _____

_____

- - - - - - - - - - - - - - - - - -

5. He hid my _____ ball.

_____

_____

- - - - - - - - - - - - - - - - - -

6. Ben _____ that fishing is fun.

_____

_____

- - - - - - - - - - - - - - - - - -

7. The _____ in the pot will get hot.

TOTAL SCORE: _____ /7

Name _____

Focus Skill: Details

▶ **Read each sentence. Fill in the circle under the picture that matches the underlined detail.**

1. The clock is <u>on the wall</u>.

 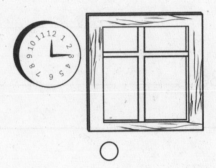

◯   ◯

2. Peg likes <u>math</u>.

 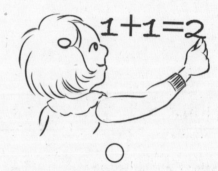

◯   ◯

3. My dog has <u>a ball</u>.

◯   ◯

Focus Skill: Details   80

4. Ken got a new <u>hat</u>.

○   ○

5. Sam digs in the <u>sand</u>.

○   ○

6. Seth's cat is <u>fat</u>.

○   ○

Focus Skill: Details

81

TOTAL SCORE: _____ /6

Name _____

Robust Vocabulary

▶ **Fill in the circle next to the correct answer.**

1. How would you feel if someone <u>applauded</u> you?

   ○ tired

   ○ upset

   ○ happy

2. If you were <u>chatty</u>, what did you do?

   ○ took a long walk

   ○ talked to a friend

   ○ fell asleep

3. If you <u>gather</u> your toys, what do you do?

   ○ bring them together in one place

   ○ throw them away

   ○ give them to your friend

4. Which one might be your <u>duty</u> as a student?

   ○ do your best

   ○ tease younger children

   ○ play video games

5. Which one might a person <u>envy</u>?

○ a person with an ice cream

○ a baby with a broken toy

○ a dog holding a muddy sock

---

6. Which one might a person <u>resent</u>?

○ Someone says thank you.

○ Someone gets in front of you.

○ Someone likes the color blue.

Grammar: Nouns: People and Places

▶ **Fill in the circle next to the correct answer.**

I. What is a noun that names some people?

The men went up the hill.

○ men   ○ went   ○ hill

2. What is a noun that names a person?

Dad swims in the pond.

○ Dad   ○ swims   ○ pond

3. What is a noun that names a place?

Beth got a hat at the mall.

○ Beth   ○ got   ○ mall

4. What is a noun that names a place?

Mom met me at the bank.

○ Mom   ○ met   ○ bank

Teacher Read-Aloud

Name _____

Weekly
Lesson Test
• • • • • • • • •
Lesson 9

Selection Comprehension

▶ **Fill in the circle next to the correct answer.**

1. The writer wants this story to

○ tell rules for a game.

○ teach about plants.

○ just make us smile.

_____

2. What do leaves make to help plants?

○ food

○ water

○ sand

_____

3. What can both people and plants do?

○ They hop.

○ They grow.

○ They jump.

_____

4. What might some plants eat?

○ fly

○ pie

○ jam

▶ **Draw or write an answer to the question.**

5. What is something else that can grow?

Name _____

Phonics/Spelling: Short vowel /u/u

▶ **Fill in the circle under the word that names each picture.**

1.

cub	us	bus
○	○	○

2.

mugs	mops	mess
○	○	○

3.

help	hump	hand
○	○	○

4.

tub	bus	tug
○	○	○

TOTAL SCORE: _____ /4

© Harcourt • Grade 1

Name _____

Phonics/Spelling: Initial Blends with *r*

▶ **Fill in the circle under the word that names each picture.**

1.

| frog | flip | fuzz |
| ○ | ○ | ○ |

2.

| drip | drum | drop |
| ○ | ○ | ○ |

3.

| cloth | crib | crab |
| ○ | ○ | ○ |

4.

| truck | thumb | thank |
| ○ | ○ | ○ |

TOTAL SCORE: _____ /4

Name _____

High-Frequency Words

▶ **Write a word from the box to complete each sentence.**

many	be	grow	does	food	live

1. She wants to _____ next to dad.

_____

2. The cat _____ not like the dog.

_____

3. There will be lots of _____ at the picnic.

_____

4. The plant will _____ to be tall.

High-Frequency Words

89

5. Mom and I _____ next to the park.

6. There are _____ fish in the pond.

Name _____

Focus Skill: Details

▶ **Read each sentence. Fill in the circle under the picture that matches the underlined detail.**

1. Pam's ball <u>hit the wall</u>.

      ○   ○

2. Jim <u>runs on the path</u>.

      ○   ○

3. Ned <u>looks at the clock</u>.

      ○   ○

Focus Skill: Details

4. Kim's pet <u>won a ribbon</u>.

○   ○

5. Mom's lamp <u>fell off the desk</u>.

○   ○

6. Beth <u>hid</u> the doll.

○   ○

Robust Vocabulary

▶ **Fill in the circle next to the correct answer.**

1. If you ate a <u>nutritious</u> snack, which one did you eat?

   ○ candy

   ○ carrots

   ○ gum

---

2. What is the <u>function</u> of a cap?

   ○ to cover a person's head

   ○ to catch a ball

   ○ to read a book

---

3. Which of these would you <u>classify</u> with an apple?

   ○ grapes

   ○ chips

   ○ pizza

4. If you <u>claimed</u> a book, what did you do?

○ returned it to the library

○ said it was yours

○ took it to the teacher

5. Which one is a place to <u>dine</u>?

○ a restaurant

○ an office

○ a library

6. If you <u>groaned</u> at someone's joke, what did you do?

○ laughed too loud

○ cried softly

○ made a deep sound

Name _____

Grammar: Nouns: Animals or Things

▶ **Fill in the circle next to the correct answer.**

1. What is a noun that names an animal?

   The dog ran to the pond.

   ○ dog   ○ ran   ○ pond

2. What is a noun that names an animal?

   The hen has six eggs.

   ○ hen   ○ laid   ○ eggs

3. What is a noun that names a thing?

   Our cat likes Mom's plant.

   ○ cat   ○ ate   ○ plant

4. What is a noun that names a thing?

   Mom picked a bud from the plant.

   ○ Mom   ○ picked   ○ bud

TOTAL SCORE: _____ /4

Selection Comprehension

▶ **Fill in the circle next to the correct answer.**

1. What makes Jill feel sad?

○ Gus runs away.

○ Fran is not her friend.

○ She cannot kick well.

2. What helps Jill play better?

○ She runs fast.

○ She kicks hard.

○ She can use her hands.

3. Which word BEST tells about Jill?

○ strong

○ mean

○ sneaky

4. How do you know Jill has strong arms?

○ She saves Gus.

○ She hangs her head.

○ She cannot kick the ball.

▶ **Draw or write an answer to the question.**

5. What is something Jill did WELL in the story?

```
┌─────────────────────────────────────────────┐
│                                             │
│                                             │
│                                             │
│                                             │
│                                             │
│                                             │
│                                             │
│                                             │
│                                             │
└─────────────────────────────────────────────┘
```

_____

- -

_____

- -

_____

- -

_____

TOTAL SCORE: _____ /4 + _____ /2

Name _____

Phonics/Spelling: Contraction *'ll*

▶ **Fill in the circle next to the words that name the underlined contraction.**

1. I'll play tag with you.

   ○ I will

   ○ It will

   ○ They will

_____

2. He'll toss the soccer ball.

   ○ I will

   ○ We will

   ○ He will

_____

3. She'll kick the ball.

   ○ You will

   ○ She will

   ○ We will

_____

4. You'll be home soon.

   ○ You will

   ○ We will

   ○ She will

TOTAL SCORE: _____ /4

High-Frequency Words

▶ **Write a word from the box to complete each sentence.**

> arms   every   feet   head   school   use   way   your

_____
----

1. I _____ a pencil, not a pen, to do my math.

_____
----

2. Kim hits a home run _____ time she is at bat.

_____
----

3. The girl held the dog in her _____.

_____

----

4. Is this the _____ to the pond?

_____

_____

----

5. You use your _____ to kick the ball
in soccer.

_____

_____

----

6. You can use your _____ in
soccer too.

_____

_____

----

7. Is this _____ backpack?

_____

_____

----

8. What _____ do they go to?

Focus Skill: Plot

▶ **Read the story. Then answer the questions.**

Once upon a time there were three ducks. They wanted to see the world.

First they went down the road to see the cow.

"Hello, Cow," they said. "Do you want to play?"

"Moo!" said the cow. "You're too young to be far from home."

The ducks went down the road again. They saw a mouse.

"Hi, Mouse," said the ducks. "Do you want to play?"

"Squeak!" said the mouse. "Go home! You're too young to be far from home."

At the end of the road they saw the pig.

"Hello, Pig," said the ducks. "Do you want to play?"

"Oink!" said the pig. "You're too young to be far from home. Let's race to your house!"

"Sure!" said the little ducks.

The pig raced the ducks all the way home.

Name _____

1. Which picture shows what happens at the beginning of the story?

○   ○   ○

_____

2. Which picture shows what happens in the middle of the story?

○   ○   ○

_____

3. Which picture shows what happens at the end of the story?

○   ○   ○

Focus Skill: Plot

TOTAL SCORE: _____ /3

© Harcourt • Grade 1

Robust Vocabulary

▶ **Fill in the circle next to the correct answer.**

1. Which one might make you feel <u>ashamed</u>?

   ○ saying something mean to your sister

   ○ reading a book on the weekend

   ○ riding a bike after school

2. If you <u>mused</u> about something, what might you have done?

   ○ carried it

   ○ thought about it

   ○ forgot about it

3. If you <u>soared</u>, which one of these would you need?

   ○ fins

   ○ wings

   ○ claws

4. Which one might make you feel <u>athletic</u>?

○ playing ball

○ hugging a baby

○ reading a book

5. What might make you feel <u>awkward</u>?

○ bumping into someone

○ looking at someone

○ talking to someone

6. Which one would most children consider a
<u>superb</u> meal?

○ snails

○ pizza

○ liver

Name _____

Grammar: One and More Than One

▶ **Fill in the circle next to the correct answer.**

1. Which noun names one?

   ○ rings

   ○ cats

   ○ girl

2. Which noun names one?

   ○ team

   ○ teams

   ○ boys

3. Which noun names more than one?

   ○ hat

   ○ hats

   ○ dog

4. Which noun names more than one?

   ○ socks

   ○ bat

   ○ cub

Grammar: One and More Than One   105   TOTAL SCORE: _____ /4

Name _____

Selection Comprehension

▶ **Fill in the circle next to the correct answer.**

1. Why did the author write "Land of Ice"?

   ○ to teach about things that live in the cold

   ○ to tell a funny story about ice

   ○ to show how to make ice

2. Which animal lives in the land of ice?

   ○ cat

   ○ fish

   ○ horse

3. Which animal lives on BOTH land and water?

   ○ penguin

   ○ whale

   ○ fish

4. What does this story have?

   ○ animals that talk

   ○ words that sound alike

   ○ things you see in the real world

▶ **Draw or write an answer to the question.**

5. What is something that lives in the land of ice?

_____
- -
_____
- -
_____
- -
_____

Phonics/Spelling: *r-* Controlled Vowel *or*, *ore*

▶ **Fill in the circle under the word that names
each picture.**

1.

corn	cob	cow
○	○	○

2.

swim	spot	storm
○	○	○

3.

short	orange	order
○	○	○

4.

horse	horn	house
○	○	○

TOTAL SCORE: _____ /4

Name _____

High-Frequency Words

▶ **Write a word from the box to complete each sentence.**

```
animals  cold  fish  from  their  under  very
```

_____
- -

1. The pencil is _____ the book.

_____

_____
- -

2. There are many _____ in the forest.

_____

_____
- - - - - - - - - - - - - - - - - - -

3. I see a big _____ in the pond.

_____

_____
- - - - - - - - - - - - - - - - - - -

4. I got a kitten _____ my dad.

High-Frequency Words

© Harcourt • Grade 1

Name _____

_____

5. The blanket is _____ soft.

_____

_____

----

6. Ben and Liz went back to _____ class.

_____

_____

----

7. Penguins live where it is _____.

TOTAL SCORE: _____ /7

Name _____

Focus Skill: Compare/Contrast

▶ **Look at the pictures and read the sentences. Fill in the circle next to the answer that tells how the things are alike.**

Pete has a pet dog.

His dog is black.

His dog likes to play with a ball.

Pete walks his dog in the park.

Pam has a pet cat.

Her cat is black.

Her cat likes to sleep.

Pam plays with her cat in the house.

Focus Skill: Compare/Contrast

I. How are Pete and Pam alike?

○ They like to sleep.

○ They own a pet.

○ They walk in the park.

2. How are the dog and the cat alike?

○ They like to sleep.

○ They like to walk.

○ They are both black.

▶ **Now tell how Pete and Pam play in different ways. Complete each sentence.**

3. Pete plays with his dog in the ____.

○ park

○ school

○ house

4. Pam plays with her cat in the ____.

○ park

○ school

○ house

Focus Skill: Compare/Contrast

112

TOTAL SCORE: _____ /4

Teacher Read-Aloud

Name _____

Weekly
Lesson Test
. . . .
Lesson 11

Robust Vocabulary

▶ **Fill in the circle next to the correct answer.**

1. Which one would help you <u>adapt</u> to living
   where it is hot?

   ○ a sweater

   ○ a fan

   ○ a car

2. Which one might you do if you thought a song
   was <u>intriguing</u>?

   ○ tell a friend to listen to the song

   ○ refuse to listen to the song again

   ○ forget about the song

3. If you had a <u>raging</u> fever, how might you feel?

   ○ kind

   ○ sick

   ○ happy

© Harcourt • Grade 1

4. Which one do penguins <u>inhabit</u>?

    ○ lakes

    ○ land of ice

    ○ desert

---

5. If you <u>pranced</u> around a room, what did you do?

    ○ strolled

    ○ skated

    ○ bounced

---

6. How might you feel if a puppy <u>nuzzled</u> you?

    ○ relaxed

    ○ afraid

    ○ upset

Name _____

Grammar: Special Names and Titles for People

▶ **Fill in the circle next to the word that answers each question.**

1. Which word is a special title for a person?

Mr. Mills has a kitten.

○ kitten   ○ Mills   ○ Mr.

---

2. Which word is a special title for a person?

Dr. Hank is Spot's vet.

○ Dr.   ○ Hank   ○ vet

---

3. Which word is a special name for a person?

Ms. Link is our coach.

○ Ms.   ○ Link   ○ coach

---

4. Which word is a special name for a person?

A bee stung Mr. Jacks.

○ Jacks   ○ Mr.   ○ bee

Selection Comprehension

▶ **Fill in the circle next to the correct answer.**

I. How does the king get gold?

    ○ He wishes for it.

    ○ He digs it up.

    ○ He finds it.

2. What happens LAST in the story?

    ○ The king wants no more gold.

    ○ The king sees a red flower.

    ○ The king picks an apple.

3. How does the king feel at the END of the story?

    ○ sad

    ○ glad

    ○ upset

4. Why could this story never happen?

    ○ Kings do not eat apples.

    ○ Kings do not have a bed.

    ○ Kings do not turn things to gold.

▶ **Draw or write an answer to the question.**

5. What part of the story did you like the BEST?

Name _____

Phonics/Spelling: Digraph *sh*

▶ **Fill in the circle under the word that names each picture.**

1.

shop   wish   shed
○   ○   ○

2.

shut   shell   ship
○   ○   ○

3.

brush   bush   block
○   ○   ○

4.

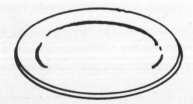

disk   dish   dash
○   ○   ○

TOTAL SCORE: _____ /4

Name _____

High-Frequency Words

▶ **Write a word from the box to complete each sentence.**

| came could gold happy made night saw were |

_____

1. Dad lost his _____ ring.

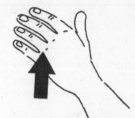

_____

2. Mom _____ a sandwich for lunch.

_____

3. We _____ going to the store.

_____

4. I like to look at the stars at _____.

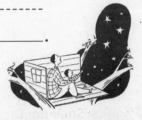

Name _____

_____

5. She _____ jump just
like her dad.

_____

6. Todd is _____ that he
got a dog.

_____

7. Jen _____ a bug in
the grass.

_____

8. Pam _____ to visit.

High-Frequency Words   120   TOTAL SCORE: _____ /8

Name _____

Focus Skill: Story Elements (Setting)

▶ **Read each sentence. Fill in the circle under the picture that shows the setting.**

1. Beth ran up the hill.

     ◯   ◯

2. Six fish swam in the pond.

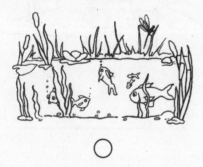   

     ◯   ◯

3. Dan saw a skunk in the forest.

     ◯   ◯

Focus Skill: Story Elements (Setting)   121

4. The dog slept in the shed.

○   ○

---

5. Kim and her Dad go to the mall.

○   ○

---

6. Tam plays in the park.

○   ○

Robust Vocabulary

▶ **Fill in the circle next to the correct answer.**

1. If someone were <u>cruel</u> to you, how might you feel?

   ○ upset

   ○ excited

   ○ happy

2. For which one might you get a <u>reward</u>?

   ○ throwing trash on the ground

   ○ finding a lost puppy

   ○ hitting your sister

3. Where might you go while dressed <u>handsomely</u>?

   ○ a pool

   ○ a wedding

   ○ a circus

4. What might you do in a <u>greedy</u> manner?

○ eat your favorite snack

○ talk to your best friend

○ watch a movie

5. What might be the <u>consequences</u> if you forget
to do your homework?

○ You will get a good grade.

○ Your teacher will be happy.

○ You will get a poor grade.

6. Which one might you <u>regret</u>?

○ yelling at your brother

○ doing well on a test

○ helping a friend

Name _____

Grammar: Special Names of Places

▶ **Fill in the answer circle next to the word or words that name the special place.**

1. **I met Jim Shaw at Barton Elementary.**

   ○ Jim Shaw

   ○ Barton Elementary

   ○ met

2. **My neighbor is moving to Oak Street.**

   ○ moving

   ○ neighbor

   ○ Oak Street

3. **Hills Park is a park that Josh likes to visit.**

   ○ Hills Park

   ○ park

   ○ Josh

4. **My family went to Mason City on vacation.**

   ○ my family

   ○ vacation

   ○ Mason City

Grammar: Special Names of Places   TOTAL SCORE: _____ /4

Selection Comprehension

▶ **Fill in the circle next to the correct answer.**

1. The writer of this story wants to

   ○ teach about a butterfly.

   ○ tell a funny butterfly story.

   ○ show how to make butterfly art.

2. Which happens FIRST?

   ○ The butterfly gets wings.

   ○ The butterfly sheds its skin.

   ○ The butterfly egg hatches.

3. How does rain help the butterfly?

   ○ It cleans the butterfly.

   ○ It gives the butterfly a drink.

   ○ It helps the butterfly fly.

4. How many legs does the butterfly have?

   ○ two

   ○ four

   ○ six

Name _____

▶ **Draw or write an answer to the question.**

5. How does the caterpillar change in the story?

[ ]

_____

- -

_____

- -

_____

- -

_____

Selection Comprehension
"A Butterfly Grows"

127

TOTAL SCORE: _____ /8 + _____ /2

Phonics/Spelling: Digraphs /ch/ *ch*, *tch*

▶ **Fill in the circle under the word that names each picture.**

1.

watch   wish   went

○   ○   ○

2.

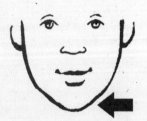

piece   catch   peace

○   ○   ○

3.

chill   chick   chain

○   ○   ○

4.

chin   chop   chip

○   ○   ○

TOTAL SCORE: _____ /4

Name _____

High-Frequency Words

▶ **Write a word from the box to complete each sentence.**

| air fly friends grew need play rain watch |

1. Britt wants to _____ tennis.

2. The plant _____ tall in the sun.

3. After playing, I _____ a glass of water.

4. The _____ is falling on the pond.

© Harcourt • Grade 1

_____
- - - - - - - - - - - - - - - - - - - -

5. I like the smell of fresh _____ .

_____
- - - - - - - - - - - - - - - - - - - -

6. I will _____ my dad fix the flat.

_____
- - - - - - - - - - - - - - - - - - - -

7. Tom has many _____ .

_____
- - - - - - - - - - - - - - - - - - - -

8. A bat can _____ at night.

Name _____

Focus Skill: Sequence

▶ **Look at the pictures. Read each group of sentences. Then fill in the circle that answers the question.**

1. What happens first?

○ The farmer plants bean seeds.

○ The farmer picks the beans.

○ The bean plants grow in the sun.

---

2. What happens next?

○ The farmer plants bean seeds.

○ The farmer picks the beans.

○ The bean plants grow in the sun.

---

3. What happens last?

○ The farmer plants bean seeds.

○ The farmer picks the beans.

○ The bean plants grow in the sun.

Focus Skill: Sequence

131

Name _____

4. What happens first?

○ Maria's dad cooks the pancakes.

○ Maria and her dad eat the pancakes.

○ Maria and her dad mix the pancakes.

5. What happens next?

○ Maria's dad cooks the pancakes.

○ Maria and her dad eat the pancakes.

○ Maria and her dad mix the pancakes.

6. What happens last?

○ Maria's dad cooks the pancakes.

○ Maria and her dad eat the pancakes.

○ Maria and her dad mix the pancakes.

Focus Skill: Sequence

132

TOTAL SCORE: _____ /6

© Harcourt • Grade 1

Weekly
Lesson Test
· · · · · · · · · · ·
Lesson 13

Robust Vocabulary

▶ **Fill in the circle next to the correct answer.**

1. What happens when you <u>examine</u> a picture?

   ○ You look at it closely.

   ○ You draw a frame around it.

   ○ You make a copy of it.

2. What happens when you <u>transform</u> water into ice?

   ○ You slowly drink it.

   ○ You change it by freezing it.

   ○ You write how you did it.

3. How might you feel before you <u>devour</u> a sandwich?

   ○ hungry

   ○ bored

   ○ sleepy

4. Which one might be <u>astonishing</u>?

    ○ eating a good breakfast

    ○ receiving a special gift

    ○ falling asleep at night

5. If you <u>continue</u> to play outdoors when it begins to rain, what might happen?

    ○ You might get wet.

    ○ You might win the game.

    ○ You might read a book.

6. Which one do you <u>doubt</u>?

    ○ A dog can fly like a bird.

    ○ The stars are out at night.

    ○ You can write with a pencil.

Grammar: Names of Days and Months

▶ **Fill in the circle next to the sentence that is written correctly.**

I. My birthday is in April.

○

Josh's birthday is in november.

○

---

2. School begins in august.

○

School ends in June.

○

---

3. The first day of the school week is monday.

○

The last day of the school week is Friday.

○

---

4. Dad makes pancakes on Saturday.

○

We go to see my grandmother on sunday.

○

Grammar: Names of Days and Months 135

TOTAL SCORE: _____ /4

© Harcourt • Grade 1

Oral Reading Fluency

Kim saw a big, black cat. It was in back of some boxes in the shed. The cat did not want to come to Kim. Then Kim sang, "Cat, cat, cat. What a cat is that? Would a cat like that want to put on my hat?"

The cat looked at Kim. She sang on. The cat kept looking. Then Kim stopped singing. The cat stopped looking.

"Come and let me pet you, " said Kim. The cat did not come.

"Do I have to sing to be your friend?" asked Kim.

Kim sang, "Cat, cat, cat, come and chat, chat, chat. Can a cat like that sit on a mat?"

The cat looked at Kim. Kim kept singing. The cat came and sat down at her feet. Kim patted the happy cat.

_____ /WCPM

Selection Comprehension

▶ **Fill in the circle next to the correct answer.**

1. Why is this Mark's big day?

   ○ He is getting a pet.

   ○ He is going to a party.

   ○ He is in a school play.

2. Mrs. Parks wants Mark to talk

   ○ louder.

   ○ sooner.

   ○ slower.

3. What happens in the play?

   ○ Mark takes a big bow.

   ○ Mark makes a mistake.

   ○ Mark does not go on stage.

4. How does Mark feel at the end of the story?

   ○ upset

   ○ happy

   ○ puzzled

Name _____

▶ **Draw or write an answer to the question.**

5. What is one thing Mark does in the story?

TOTAL SCORE: _____ /4 + _____ /2

Name _____

Phonics/Spelling: -r controlled vowel /är/ ar

▶ **Fill in the circle under the word that names each picture.**

1.

card	car	cash
○	○	○

2.

barn	bran	bank
○	○	○

3.

ant	art	arm
○	○	○

4.

star	stamp	start
○	○	○

TOTAL SCORE: _____ /4

High-Frequency Words

▶ **Write a word from the box to complete each sentence.**

| again | feel | house | know | loud | Mrs. | put | say |

1. _____ Scott plays with her dog.

2. My _____ is next to the school.

3. The alarm has a _____ bell.

4. Dennis _____ the kitten in the box.

5. Miss Parks sang the song _____ .

---

6. I like to _____ happy.

---

7. What did she _____ to Miss Smith?

---

8. Do you _____ Ed?

Focus Skill: Author's Purpose/ Point of View

▶ **Read the story. Fill in the circle next to the correct answer.**

Oak trees grow in many different places. Some trees grow in warm places. Some trees grow in places that have cold, snowy winters. There are more than 200 kinds of oak trees.

White oaks grow very tall. They may get as high as 150 feet. The trunk of a white oak can be 8 feet thick.

Black oaks are often smaller than white oaks. New black oaks have gray bark. Their bark turns to black as they get older.

I. What is the author's purpose?

○ to play

○ to entertain

○ to teach

2. How do you know that this story is about something in real life?

- ○ Oak trees are real.
- ○ The trees can sing.
- ○ I know a song about oak trees.

---

3. How do you think the author feels about oak trees?

- ○ The author thinks oak trees are interesting.
- ○ The author does not like oak trees.
- ○ The author likes pine trees better than oak trees.

Name _____

Robust Vocabulary

▶ **Fill in the circle next to the correct answer.**

1. If you <u>approached</u> a starting line, what did you do?

   ○ walked toward it

   ○ walked away from it

   ○ walked along it

2. Which might make you <u>energetic</u>?

   ○ watching television

   ○ playing video games

   ○ eating a healthful snack

3. What kind of <u>pace</u> would be best for a short race?

   ○ very fast

   ○ as slow as possible

   ○ not too fast

4. Which one is a <u>blunder</u> you might make?

○ spilling milk

○ weeding a garden

○ taking a walk

---

5. Which one might you say to <u>reassure</u> a friend?

○ "Why did you do that?"

○ "Uh-oh."

○ "That's all right."

---

6. If you <u>excel</u> in playing soccer, what can you do?

○ play well

○ play poorly

○ not play at all

Robust Vocabulary

TOTAL SCORE: _____ /6

Name _____

Grammar: Names of Holidays

▶ **Fill in the circle next to the name of a holiday.**

1. We march with flags on the Fourth of July.
   - ○ We march
   - ○ with flags
   - ○ Fourth of July

2. We give thanks on Thanksgiving Day.
   - ○ thanks on
   - ○ We give
   - ○ Thanksgiving Day

3. Pam made a card for Mother's Day.
   - ○ Mother's Day
   - ○ Pam made
   - ○ a card

4. Beth wore a red dress on Valentine's Day.
   - ○ red dress
   - ○ Valentine's Day
   - ○ Beth

Grammar: Names of Holidays   146   TOTAL SCORE: _____ /4

Oral Reading Fluency

I like to look at the stars. I do it often. I know many of their names. They shift a little bit from night to night.

Last night I saw a new star.

It was big and it was beautiful. I looked at the new star far into the night.

Do you look at the stars? Did you see a new one? Was it the biggest star you saw last night?

I want to name the new star I saw last night. Can we give it a name?

Do you think this star is there just for you?

Name _____

Selection Comprehension

▶ **Fill in the circle next to the correct answer.**

1. How does Grandpa help the children have fun?

   ○ He plays games.

   ○ He tells stories.

   ○ He makes snacks.

2. What does Grandpa tell Tomás to do?

   ○ work hard

   ○ go to school

   ○ read a lot

3. What is this story mostly about?

   ○ Tomás was born in Texas.

   ○ Tomás likes to read and write stories.

   ○ Tomás and his family went to a farm.

4. Tomás Rivera's name is on a library because

   ○ he became a writer.

   ○ wanted to be a builder.

   ○ he was a farmer.

▶ **Draw or write an answer to the question.**

5. Tomás liked to read lots of books. What is something you like to read or hear stories about?

Phonics/Spelling: Digraphs /kw/*qu* /hw/*wh*

▶ **Fill in the circle under the word that names each picture.**

1.

quest   quiz   queen
○   ○   ○

2.

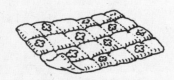

quilt   quit   quack
○   ○   ○

3.

while   whale   whack
○   ○   ○

4.

wheel   whiz   whip
○   ○   ○

TOTAL SCORE: _____ /4

Phonics/Spelling: Inflections -*ed*, *ing* (double final consonant)

▶ **Fill in the circle next to the word that completes each sentence.**

1. Jason _____ at every house.

   ○ stooped

   ○ stopped

   ○ stoped

2. Dad _____ to the park at sunset.

   ○ jogged

   ○ joged

   ○ joging

3. Scarlet _____ in the mud and fell.

   ○ skided

   ○ skidded

   ○ skidding

4. The frog _____ into the pond.

   ○ hoped

   ○ hoping

   ○ hopped

High-Frequency Words

▶ **Write a word from the box to complete each sentence.**

> about books family name people read work writing

_____
- - - - - - - - - - - - - - - - - - -
1. She is _____ to her pal Sam.

_____
- - - - - - - - - - - - - - - -
2. Greg read a book _____ cats.

_____
- - - - - - - - - - - - - - - - - -
3. How many _____ are in this family?

4. My dad grills chicken for all of

_____
- - - - - - - - - - - - - - - - -
the _____.

5. Mom picked me up after _____.

_____

6. I can _____ the problem.

_____

7. Mrs. Gil will _____ her new kitten.

_____

8. Our class is reading the _____ on the first shelf.

TOTAL SCORE: _____ /8

© Harcourt • Grade 1

Name _____

Focus Skill: Sequence

▶ **Look at the pictures. Read each group of
sentences. Then fill in the circle that answers
the question.**

1. What happens first?

○ You put jam on the muffin.

○ You eat the muffin.

○ You get a muffin from mom.

---

2. What happens next?

○ You put jam on the muffin.

○ You eat the muffin.

○ You get a muffin.

---

3. What happens last?

○ You put jam on the muffin.

○ You eat the muffin.

○ You get a muffin.

Focus Skill: Sequence

154

Name _____

4. What happens first?

○ The robin sits on her nest.

○ The eggs in the nest hatch.

○ The robin feeds the little birds.

5. What happens next?

○ The robin sits on her nest.

○ The eggs in the nest hatch.

○ The robin feeds the little birds.

6. What happens last?

○ The robin sits on her nest.

○ The eggs in the nest hatch.

○ The robin feeds the little birds.

Focus Skill: Sequence

155

TOTAL SCORE: _____ /6

Name _____

Robust Vocabulary

▶ **Fill in the circle next to the correct answer.**

I. In which of the following would you sit <u>cozily</u>?

○ a soft couch

○ a hard chair

○ a bench

2. What do you say to someone you have <u>interrupted</u>?

○ "Good morning."

○ "Thank you."

○ "Excuse me."

3. After which one might you act <u>triumphantly</u>?

○ winning a big game

○ forgetting your homework

○ reading with a friend

4. Which one is an <u>accomplishment</u> you might like to achieve?

   ○ going to sleep at night

   ○ becoming a leader in your class

   ○ reading your name

5. If people say that they <u>admire</u> you, how would you feel?

   ○ proud

   ○ unhappy

   ○ tired

6. Which one is an <u>ambition</u> you might have?

   ○ teaching a duck to sing

   ○ playing a musical instrument

   ○ forgetting your backpack

Name _____

Grammar: Using *I* and *Me*

▶ **Fill in the circle next to the word that completes the sentence.**

1. Dad reads to _____.

    ◯ I

    ◯ me

2. Helen and _____ like to bring our lunch to school.

    ◯ I

    ◯ me

3. Call _____ in the morning.

    ◯ I

    ◯ me

4. Jack and _____ ran on the track.

    ◯ I

    ◯ me

Grammar: Using *I* and *Me*

TOTAL SCORE: _____ /4

Oral Reading Fluency

A big, black cat hid by the buckets on the porch. Kim came to sit on the porch. The cat crept to Kim. Crash! The cat landed not far from Kim. Kim started to sing, "Cat, cat, cat. What a cat is that? Will a cat ask for my hat?"

The cat started to go to Kim. Kim sang on. The cat kept going. Then Kim stopped singing. The cat stopped.

"Oh, cat," said Kim. "Come and let me pat your head." The cat stopped.

"Do I have to sing to be your pal?" asked Kim.

Kim sang some more. "Cat, cat, cat, come and chat, chat, chat. Can a cat like that swing a bat?" The cat started to go to Kim again. Kim kept singing. The cat sat next to Kim's feet.

159

_____ /WCPM

Selection Comprehension

▶ **Fill in the circle next to the correct answer.**

I. Ant asks other animals to

- ○ rest with her.
- ○ eat with her.
- ○ play a game with her.

2. The LAST animal Ant invites is very

- ○ big.
- ○ old.
- ○ short.

3. What does the story teach us?

- ○ to save money
- ○ to work hard
- ○ to be a friend

4. Why could this story never happen?

- ○ Frogs do not hop.
- ○ Ants do not talk.
- ○ Dogs do not run.

Name _____

▶ **Draw or write an answer to the question.**

5. What happens in the END of the story?

_____

- -

_____

- -

_____

- -

Selection Comprehension
"One More Friend"

161

TOTAL SCORE: _____ /4 + _____ /2

Name _____

Phonics/Spelling: r-controlled vowels /ûr/ er, ir, ur

▶ **Fill in the circle under the word that names each picture.**

1.

    bird   bus   bring
    ◯   ◯   ◯

2.

    fall   food   fur
    ◯   ◯   ◯

3.

    from   fern   fish
    ◯   ◯   ◯

4.

    got   girl   get
    ◯   ◯   ◯

Phonics/Spelling: r-controlled vowels
/ûr/ er, ir, ur

TOTAL SCORE: _____ /4

High-Frequency Words

▶ **Write a word from the box to complete each sentence.**

always	by	cow's	join	nice	please	room

1. _____ _____ give Jed his backpack.

2. Pam kept her dolls in her _____
_____.

3. Dad _____ helps with
the dishes.

_____
----

4. The _____ spots are black.

_____
----

5. Will you stop _____ the
sports shop?

_____
----

6. Don will _____ us for
lunch.

_____
----

7. My pal Sam is very _____.

© Harcourt • Grade 1

Name _____

Focus Skill: Main Idea

▶ **Read the story. Fill in the circles next to the correct answers.**

Grandma says she will show me how to make her special tea. No one else at home knows how to make it. This makes me feel good.

First, she makes the water very hot. Then, she uses a spoon to get the tea out of the jar. She puts four spoons of tea and the hot water into a pretty pot.

We must wait until the tea is just right. Last, we stir in a little sugar. No one knows about this step! Grandma shows me how much sugar to use.

When I get older, I will make tea by myself. Now, I like to watch Grandma and keep her secret.

I. What is the main idea?

○ The speaker loves tea.

○ Grandma shows how to make her special tea.

○ The speaker wants to make tea.

Focus Skill: Main Idea

2. What does Grandma do first?

○ stirs in sugar

○ puts tea in the pot

○ heats the water

---

3. Which step is secret?

○ heating the water

○ adding the sugar

○ pouring the tea

---

4. How much tea does Grandma use?

○ four spoons

○ two spoons

○ three spoons

Focus Skill: Main Idea

TOTAL SCORE: _____ /4

Robust Vocabulary

▶ **Fill in the circle next to the correct answer.**

1. Which one might you <u>struggle</u> to do?

   ○ push a heavy chair across a room

   ○ lift a feather with your fingers

   ○ pick a flower from a garden

2. If you <u>captured</u> a bug, what did you do?

   ○ killed it

   ○ caught it

   ○ gave it away

3. How might you show another person <u>mercy</u>?

   ○ You forgive them for doing wrong.

   ○ You finish your homework.

   ○ You feel that they are older than you.

4. With which ones are you <u>compatible</u>?

   ○ snakes

   ○ friends

   ○ bees

5. To which one might you go to <u>relax</u>?

○ the doctor

○ a vet

○ a library

_____

6. If someone says you are <u>amiable</u>, you are

○ friendly.

○ upset.

○ bored.

Grammar: Using *He, She, It, and They*

▶ **Fill in the circle next to the word that can take the place of the underlined word or words.**

1. The <u>windmill</u> spins in the storm.
   - ○ She
   - ○ It
   - ○ They

2. <u>Pam</u> cracked an egg.
   - ○ She
   - ○ He
   - ○ It

3. The <u>men</u> went on a trip.
   - ○ They
   - ○ She
   - ○ He

4. <u>Bart</u> wants to sing.
   - ○ They
   - ○ He
   - ○ It

Grammar: *Using He, She, It and They*   169   TOTAL SCORE: _____ /4

Oral Reading Fluency

Fred the fish was bored. Every day he swam in the pond. He swam fast. He swam on his back. He swam with one fin. He swam with two fins.

Then he met a frog sitting on a rock in the sun. Her name was Pam. Pam was bored, too.

Fred asked Pam to swim with him.

Pam said, "Frogs hop. Hop with me."

Fred said, "Fish just swim."

"Frogs can swim, too," Pam said. She hopped into the water. Fred and Pam swam in the pond.

Every day, Fred and Pam played. Fred had fun. Pam did, too.

Then they met an otter. His name was Quinn. Pam asked Quinn to play with them.

Quinn said, "Playing is fun."

Quinn, Pam, and Fred had fun. Fred was glad to have pals.

Name _____

Selection Comprehension

▶ **Fill in the circle next to the correct answer.**

1. Why do the elephants need a new job?

○ The trees are all cut.

○ The farm is moving.

○ The work is too hard.

2. Why does Alex want the elephants to paint?

○ to show how they feel

○ to make money

○ to have fun

3. How are Alex and the elephants the SAME?

○ They all have hands.

○ They all have trunks.

○ They all can paint.

4. What does this story have?

○ elephants that are real

○ words that sound alike

○ elephants that can talk

TOTAL SCORE: _____ /

▶ **Draw or write an answer to the question.**

5. What is one thing the elephants do in this story?

Name _____

High-Frequency Words

▶ **Write a word from the box to complete each sentence.**

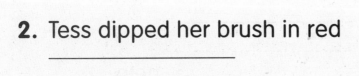

| buy | carry | money | other | paint | paper | would |

1. Dennis forgot his _____ for lunch.

2. Tess dipped her brush in red
   _____
   _____.

3. Elmer will _____ the books
   in his backpack.

4. Doris and Beth put

_____

_____ in a trash can.

---

5. An egg is in the pan. The

_____

_____ egg has a crack.

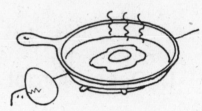

_____

----

6. Sal asked Jim if he _____ help.

_____

----

7. Pat will _____ an apple for lunch.

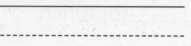

Focus Skill: Main Idea

▶ **Read the story. Fill in the circles next to the correct answers.**

The baby bird was afraid. He was sure that he did not know how to fly, but his mother did not seem to agree with him.

Little by little, his mother pushed him closer to the edge of the nest. "I am not ready," the baby bird said. "Please, mother, do not push me out of this nest!"

Her face looked kind, but the mother just kept pushing. She knew the time was right. She could not tell her son this. He would have to learn it for himself.

The baby bird began to fall, and the ground seemed very close. At the last moment, he soared up high. He could fly!

I. What is the main idea of this story?

○ The baby bird was afraid.

○ Birds live in nests.

○ The mother bird knew best.

2. Why did the baby bird's mother push him out of the nest?

○ She knew that he could fly.

○ She wanted more space.

○ She did not know she pushed him.

---

3. Why was the baby bird afraid?

○ He knew how to fly.

○ He loved his nest.

○ He did not want to fall.

---

4. What was the last thing that happened in the story?

○ The baby bird was pushed from the nest.

○ The baby bird fell asleep.

○ The baby bird began to fly.

Focus Skill: Main Idea

TOTAL SCORE: _____ /4

Name _____

Robust Vocabulary

▶ **Fill in the circle next to the correct answer.**

1. If you are in a <u>predicament</u>, how might you feel?

   ○ happy

   ○ worried

   ○ bored

2. Which one would make you <u>rejoice</u>?

   ○ some good news

   ○ a poor grade

   ○ a silly story

3. Which one describes something <u>extraordinary</u>?

   ○ children laughing

   ○ elephants dancing

   ○ birds singing

4. Which one might go <u>unnoticed</u>?

○ the principal juggling

○ a monkey in your class

○ a flea on a pet

5. How might you feel if a friend broke an <u>agreement</u> with you?

○ happy

○ sad

○ tired

6. Which one might be <u>unthinkable</u> in your classroom?

○ reading a story

○ drawing on paper

○ throwing a ball

Grammar: Possessives

▶ **Choose the word that shows ownership.**

1. Seth's hands fit into the mittens.

   ○ Seth's

   ○ hands

   ○ mittens

2. The girl's books were on the desk.

   ○ girl's

   ○ books

   ○ desk

3. The puppet is theirs.

   ○ puppet

   ○ theirs

   ○ is

4. Her backpack is on the bed.

   ○ bed

   ○ backpack

   ○ Her

Oral Reading Fluency

Rob and his sister Beth got lost. They went on a path that Rob said was a shortcut. They shuffled on the path.

Beth stepped on a twig. It snapped.

"Can we go back?" Beth asked.

Rob sat on a stump. He was upset.

"I never get lost," Rob said.

"I wish we had a map," Beth said.

Beth sat on the dirt. She looked in her backpack. She had drinks and snacks. Beth and Rob had a picnic. Beth had a sandwich. Rob had an apple.

A squirrel ran by. A frog hopped by. It started getting dark. Rob felt bad. Beth patted his hand.

Mom called from the path. Beth and Rob ran to her. "We got lost," Beth said. Mom hugged them.

_____ /WCPM

Selection Comprehension

▶ **Fill in the circle next to the correct answer.**

1. When does the story take place?

   ○ winter

   ○ summer

   ○ spring

---

2. The author of the story wants to

   ○ tell a funny story.

   ○ teach why it snows.

   ○ show how to make a snow flake.

---

3. Why does Sport jump on the snowman?

   ○ He thinks it is a real man.

   ○ He tries to get Joan's scarf.

   ○ He wants to chase birds away.

---

4. What does Ben think the snow surprise is?

   ○ a crow

   ○ a mouse

   ○ a man

Selection Comprehension
"Snow Surprise"

Name _____

▶ **Draw or write an answer to the question.**

5. What will Joan make the next time it snows?

_____

- -

_____

- -

_____

- -

TOTAL SCORE: _____ /4 + _____ /2

Phonics/Spelling: Long Vowel
/ō/ow, oa

▶ **Fill in the circle under the word that names each picture.**

1.

bird   boat   blow
○   ○   ○

2.

crow   club   crop
○   ○   ○

3.

room   road   ring
○   ○   ○

4.

boast   boss   bowl
○   ○   ○

TOTAL SCORE: _____ /4

High-Frequency Words

▶ **Write a word from the box to complete each sentence.**

| mouse   our   over   pretty   surprise   three |

1. All _____ cats sat on the porch.

2. Her new dress is _____.

3. His cat can catch a _____.

© Harcourt • Grade 1

4. The gift for Chad was a

_____

_____.

5. Ted and I follow _____ dad.

6. A lamp fell _____ when Tucker
bumped it.

Focus Skill: Author's Purpose/ Point of View

▶ **Read the story. Fill in the circle next to the correct answer.**

Gus and Mack are two black cats. Gus sings all day. Mack sits in the sun.

"Quit singing," Mack said to Gus. "Cats don't sing. Cats sit in the sun and purr."

Gus turned his head and kept singing. He sang happy songs by the window.

Birds came to the window. The birds sang along. Gus had fun singing with the birds.

The following day, more animals came to the window. Gus saw the animals. He sang a new song.

Mack came to the window. He grinned at Gus. "Cats can sing," he said. "As long as they sing in the sun."

Gus and Mack sang a happy song.

Name _____

1. What is the author's purpose?

   ○ to tell about cats

   ○ to have fun reading

   ○ to teach

2. How do you know that this story could not happen in real life?

   ○ Cats sit by the window.

   ○ Birds sing.

   ○ Cats sing.

3. How do you think the author feels about cats?

   ○ The author likes cats.

   ○ The author does not like cats.

   ○ The author likes dogs better than cats.

4. How do you think Gus feels about singing?

   ○ He loves singing.

   ○ He does not like singing.

   ○ He is mad that Mack sings.

**Focus Skill: Author's Purpose/
Point of View**

© Harcourt • Grade 1

187

TOTAL SCORE: _____ /4

Robust Vocabulary

▶ **Fill in the circle next to the correct answer.**

1. If someone gives you a <u>command</u>, they would

    ○ make a snack for you.

    ○ tell you what to do.

    ○ sit with you at lunch.

2. Which one is a topic that some people <u>argue</u> about?

    ○ which sports team is the best

    ○ what time it is

    ○ if it is raining

3. If you <u>labored</u> to finish a task, how did you work?

    ○ very little

    ○ very hard

    ○ very fast

4. Which sound would make you <u>wary</u> of entering
   a room?

   ○ a growling noise

   ○ a person singing

   ○ a kitten purring

---

5. If you <u>jostle</u> someone, where might you be?

   ○ in a crowded store

   ○ in an empty room

   ○ sitting at your desk

---

6. Which one might make your pocket <u>bulge</u>?

   ○ a penny

   ○ a paper clip

   ○ an apple

Grammar: Troublesome Words: Homophones

▶ **Choose the two words that are homophones.**

1. The girl in the red shirt read the book aloud.

- ○ girl, red
- ○ red, read
- ○ read, book

2. He would cut the wood to make a birdhouse.

- ○ would, wood
- ○ would, cut
- ○ wood, house

3. I sent Ellen a stamp that cost one cent.

- ○ sent, stamp
- ○ sent, cent
- ○ cost, cent

4. She will show us the right way to write a letter.

- ○ show, right
- ○ way, write
- ○ right, write

Oral Reading Fluency

Doris ran fast to catch the bus, but the bus left. Doris has a problem. Doris must get to class. Mrs. Miller will miss her. Doris never misses class.

Doris sits on a bench. Doris thinks to herself.

Can she run? Class is far. Doris cannot run.

Can she paddle a boat? Doris cannot paddle a boat.

Can she fly in a blimp? Doris cannot fly.

Doris can swim. Can she swim to class? Doris cannot swim to class.

Cars are fast. Can Doris go to class in a car?

Doris's dad has a car. Doris runs to her dad.

"Did you miss the bus?" he asks.

"Yes," Doris says.

Dad chuckles. "I will bring you to class," he says.

Name _____

Selection Comprehension

▶ **Fill in the circle next to the correct answer.**

1. What makes Little Rabbit think the sky is falling?

○ A friend tells him.

○ Something hits him.

○ The sky looks dark to him.

2. What happens LAST?

○ Little Rabbit hops to warn others.

○ Mother says an apple hit Little Rabbit.

○ Little Rabbit and friends eat dinner.

3. How does Little Rabbit feel at the END?

○ happy

○ upset

○ mean

4. This story could never happen because

○ rabbits can't speak.

○ rabbits can't hop.

○ rabbits can't eat.

▶ **Draw or write an answer to the question.**

5. What will Little Rabbit do the next time an apple hits him?

TOTAL SCORE: _____ /4 + _____ /2

Phonics/Spelling: Long Vowel /ē/e, ee, ea

▶ **Fill in the circle under the word that names each picture.**

1.

eagle   eager   eel

  ○   ○   ○

2.

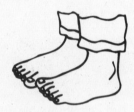

feel   feet   felt

  ○   ○   ○

3.

tea   teal   team

  ○   ○   ○

4.

tree   teen   trip

  ○   ○   ○

TOTAL SCORE: _____ /4

Phonics/Spelling: Contractions 've, 're

▶ **Fill in the circle next to the words that tell what the underlined word means.**

1. They've read this book.

○ They were

○ They have

○ They are

---

2. I've sang this song.

○ I have

○ You have

○ I am

---

3. We're going to the mall.

○ We are

○ We have

○ They are

---

4. Hal tells me that you're entering the contest.

○ You are

○ You will

○ You have

Phonics/Spelling: Contractions 've, 're   195   TOTAL SCORE: _____ /4

Name _____

High-Frequency Words

▶ **Write a word from the box to complete each sentence.**

```
dear  door  hurry  mother  should  sky  told
```

_____
----
1. We must _____ to pack.

_____

_____
----
2. Oh, _____! Meg forgot
her backpack.

_____

3. Can you see that jet in the

_____

_____?

_____

© Harcourt • Grade 1

4. Frank and Sam _____
help Miss Albert.

5. Ben helps his _____ fix lunch.

6. Seth runs out and the _____
slams shut.

7. Robert _____ us a story.

Focus Skill: Cause and Effect

▶ **Read the story. Fill in the circles next to the correct answers.**

Puff the Penguin is in trouble. Puff always eats too many fish. He eats fish all day. Now, Puff is too big for his belt. He can't get his belt to buckle and soon he has to go to his friend's sleep over. He will miss the sleep over!

Puff knows what to do. He has to eat less fish. After a week, he can just about buckle his belt.

Puff knows that he needs to swim every day, too. At first, Puff thinks that eating fish is more fun than swimming. Then Puff starts having fun swimming. He sees many of his friends when he swims. Puff and his friends have fun.

On the day of the sleep over, Puff puts on his belt. It is a perfect fit. Puff is happy to go to his friend's sleep over.

Name _____

1. Why does Puff grow too big for his belt?

   ○ He has to go to a sleep over.

   ○ He swims every day.

   ○ He eats too many fish.

2. What happens when Puff eats less fish?

   ○ Puff can just about buckle his belt.

   ○ Puff meets many friends.

   ○ Puff goes to a friend's sleep over.

3. Where does Puff go at the end of the story?

   ○ to buy a new belt

   ○ to the market for fish

   ○ to his friend's sleep over

Focus Skill: Cause and Effect

199

TOTAL SCORE: _____ /3

Robust Vocabulary

▶ **Fill in the circle next to the correct answer.**

1. Which one moves <u>rapidly</u>?

○ a snail

○ a rabbit

○ a turtle

2. Which one would you say if you were being <u>courteous</u>?

○ "Thank you."

○ "Give me that."

○ "It's my turn!"

3. If you do something <u>devious</u>, what might happen?

○ You might win a prize.

○ You might clean your room.

○ You might get in trouble.

4. Which one is an <u>unreasonable</u> chore?

○ feeding a pet

○ cleaning your room

○ building a new house

5. Which one would cause you to move <u>hastily</u>?

○ running in a race

○ a purring kitten

○ a singing teacher

6. If someone called you <u>gullible</u>, what did you do?

○ fed some birds

○ believed something silly

○ swallowed too fast

Robust Vocabulary

201

TOTAL SCORE: _____ /6

Name _____

Grammar: Describing Words: Color, Size, and Shape

▶ **Fill in the circle next to each describing word.**

1. My teacher has a red dress.

   ○ teacher

   ○ red

   ○ dress

2. That is a big bug.

   ○ That

   ○ big

   ○ bug

3. Bring me the yellow flag.

   ○ Bring

   ○ yellow

   ○ flag

4. The black shirt is my sister's.

   ○ black

   ○ shirt

   ○ sister's

TOTAL SCORE: _____ /4

Oral Reading Fluency

Miss Sanchez had a fun lunch planned for her class at school.

She asked the children to bring food for their friends.

First, Chad eats Pat's peanut butter. Then Pat drinks Rob's tea. Rob passed his napkin to Kathleen. She said thanks.

Dean let Greg have his oatmeal. It was hot. Greg handed Dean his sandwich.

Dennis bit into a radish. Gwen had an apple tart. Tucker got a pickle.

Miss Sanchez mixed Kevin's eggs with Jeff's jam.

"That was good," Chad said.

The other children had a good time too.

"It was fun," said Kathleen.

"I'll never forget it," Dean giggled. "I'm full!"

"Let's do this again," Pat said.

Miss Sanchez was glad.

Selection Comprehension

▶ **Fill in the circle next to the correct answer.**

1. What is this story about?

   ○ People live in many lands.

   ○ Sometimes it rains for weeks.

   ○ People dress in hats and coats.

2. What will you see where it is hot and dry?

   ○ homes up on stilts

   ○ homes with mud bricks

   ○ homes made of packed snow

3. You should read this story

   ○ just to have fun.

   ○ to find out about other places.

   ○ to find out how to out up a tent.

4. People in ALL the places like to

   ○ sail and swim.

   ○ catch fish.

   ○ have fun.

Name _____

▶ **Draw or write an answer to the question.**

5. If you could live in any of the places, where would you live?

```
┌────────────────────────────────────────────┐
│                                            │
│                                            │
│                                            │
│                                            │
│                                            │
│                                            │
│                                            │
│                                            │
│                                            │
└────────────────────────────────────────────┘
```

_____

- -

_____

- -

_____

- -

_____

Selection Comprehension
"Ways People Live"

TOTAL SCORE: _____ /4 + _____ /2

Name _____

Phonics/Spelling: Long Vowel /ā/ai, ay

▶ **Fill in the circle under the word that names each picture.**

1.

rain   rail   raft

○   ○   ○

2.

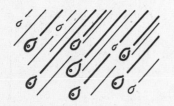

dash   dip   day

○   ○   ○

3.

plan   play   plot

○   ○   ○

4.

trash   train   trail

○   ○   ○

TOTAL SCORE: _____ /4

High-Frequency Words

▶ **Write a word from the box to complete each sentence.**

> cool   dry   holes   four   move   place   warm

1. Jeff's shirt has two _____.

2. Karl and Peg _____ the drum.

3. Beth's attic is _____ in the summer.

4. The desert is _____ and hot.

5. Mick and Jen see _____ birds in the tree.

6. The water is _____ on my hand.

7. Chester thinks that the best _____ to read is in his room.

High-Frequency Words

TOTAL SCORE: _____ /7

© Harcourt • Grade 1

Name _____

Focus Skill: Cause and Effect

▶ **Read the story. Fill in the circle next to the correct answer.**

Bess was upset. Her hamster, Bert, was not in his box.

Bess saw that the top of his box was up. That must be how Bert got away.

Bess had asked Chad to feed Bert. Chad must have left the box top up. She was not upset with Chad, but she was sad. Chad offered to help Bess find Bert.

She did not know where she would find Bert. Bert was not under the bed. Bert was not on the desk. Chad went to ask their mom and dad if they had seen Bert.

Bess sat on the bed to think. She saw her backpack move. It must be Bert! At last, she had him back.

Bert went to sleep as soon as he was back in his box. Bess shut the top of the box. She was glad to have Bert back.

1. Why does Bert get out of the box?

○ Bess is upset.

○ His box top was up.

○ He hid in a backpack.

2. What happens after the box top is up?

○ Chad offers to help.

○ Bess is upset with Chad.

○ Bert stays in his box.

3. What helps Bess to find Bert?

○ Her mother has seen him.

○ Her backpack moves.

○ Chad helps her.

4. What happens to Bert when Bess finds him?

○ Bess puts him in his box.

○ Bess gives him something to eat.

○ Bess shows him to Chad.

Focus Skill: Cause and Effect

TOTAL SCORE: _____ /4

Weekly
Lesson Test
· · · · · · · · · · · ·
Lesson 20

Robust Vocabulary

▶ **Fill in the circle next to the correct answer.**

I. Which one would you be <u>chided</u> for?

   ○ being late for school

   ○ doing your homework

   ○ taking out the trash

2. If you are <u>grumbling</u> about rainy weather,
   how do you feel?

   ○ surprised

   ○ bored

   ○ unhappy

3. Which one would you do for <u>amusement</u>?

   ○ do your homework

   ○ play with a friend

   ○ clean your room

Name _____

4. Which one is a <u>dwelling</u>?

- ○ piano
- ○ snake
- ○ house

---

5. If it were <u>bitterly</u> cold outside, what might you wear?

- ○ gloves and a scarf
- ○ sunglasses and a swimsuit
- ○ shorts and a sweater

---

6. What might happen if you <u>realized</u> that you lost your backpack?

- ○ You might have to redo your homework.
- ○ You might have to take a walk.
- ○ You might have to play games.

© Harcourt • Grade 1

Name _____

Grammar: Describing Words: Taste, Smell, Sound, and Feel

▶ **Fill in the circle next to each describing word.**

1. The kitten's fur felt soft.

- ○ soft
- ○ kitten's
- ○ felt

---

2. This lemon is sour.

- ○ lemon
- ○ is
- ○ sour

---

3. We can hear the truck's loud horn.

- ○ hear
- ○ truck's
- ○ loud

---

4. In summer, a sweet smell is in the air.

- ○ summer
- ○ sweet
- ○ smell

Grammar: Describing Words: Taste, Smell, [213]
Sound, and Feel

TOTAL SCORE: _____ /4

Oral Reading Fluency

Dean and Greg went camping with Dean's dad in a forest on Thursday.

For lunch, they had sandwiches.

They saw squirrels, rabbits, and turtles. They looked for bugs under rocks and saw a snail. They played leapfrog and tag.

Dean and Greg had fun fishing in the pond with Dean's dad. Greg had a small sailboat. He and Dean played with it in the water.

Then Greg saw a raindrop.

"We will get wet!" he yelled.

They put on their raincoats and stayed in the tent.

When it got dark, they were snug in the tent near a big fir tree. They each had a sleeping bag. It thundered and stormed.

The following day, Dean and Greg played in the puddles.

"Camping is fun," Greg said.

Selection Comprehension

▶ **Fill in the circle next to the correct answer.**

I. Where does Flake live?

○ on a farm

○ in a school

○ in a pet shop

2. What happens to Flake?

○ He runs away.

○ He falls in the trash.

○ He hides under a desk.

3. Flake comes back because he wants to

○ eat.

○ play.

○ sleep.

4. How are the children the SAME?

○ They are all girls.

○ They all look for Flake.

○ They all run on a wheel.

Name _____

▶ **Draw or write an answer to the question.**

5. What will Flake do next?

Selection Comprehension
"Flake, the Missing Hamster"

TOTAL SCORE: _____ /4 + _____ /2

© Harcourt • Grade 1

Phonics/Spelling: Long Vowel /ā/ *a-e*

▶ **Fill in the circle under the word that names each picture.**

1.

    ate   ape   and

    ○   ○   ○

2.

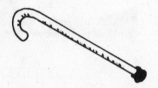

    can   came   cane

    ○   ○   ○

3.

    gate   late   get

    ○   ○   ○

4.

    let   late   lake

    ○   ○   ○

TOTAL SCORE: _____ /4

Name _____

High-Frequency Words

▶ **Write a word from the box to complete each sentence.**

around	found	gone	hears
might	near	open	tired

1. Tim runs _____ the track.

2. Bess _____ the alarm
and wakes up.

3. Brent _____ his lost
sock.

© Harcourt • Grade 1

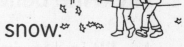

4. It is so cold that it _____ snow.

5. Mort's desk is _____ Pam's desk.

6. Peg's pet bird is _____!

7. The door was left _____, and the
bird has flown away.

8. Wilbur was _____ after the game.

High-Frequency Words

TOTAL SCORE: _____ /8

Focus Skill: Problem/Solution

▶ **Read along as your teacher reads each problem. Then circle the better solution.**

1. **Jill is playing in the park on a hot day. She is very thirsty and needs a drink. Fill in the answer circle under the picture that shows the solution to Jill's problem.**

    ○   ○

2. **May's dog Giggle is getting fat. The vet says that Giggle needs to lose weight. Fill in the answer circle under the picture that shows the solution to May and Giggle's problem.**

    ○   ○

3. **Ben and Dale sit at the same table in art class. Dale has a big box of paints. Ben has just a few paints. Fill in the answer circle under the picture that shows the solution to Ben's problem.**

○   ○

4. **Gwen and her family go on a picnic to a park. They swim in a lake. Gwen's dad sees the sky turn dark. Fill in the answer circle under the picture that shows the solution to their problem.**

○   ○

Focus Skill: Problem/Solution

TOTAL SCORE: _____ /4

Robust Vocabulary

▶ **Fill in the circle next to the correct answer.**

I. Which one might you be <u>alarmed</u> to hear?

○ a loud crash

○ a baby's laugh

○ a favorite song

---

2. Which one might you be <u>overjoyed</u> to receive?

○ a dirty shoe

○ a bag of trash

○ a surprise gift

---

3. Which one might you find <u>mysterious</u>?

○ a package without a card

○ a walk with your friend

○ a game of football

---

4. Which one is a way you might show <u>sympathy</u>?

○ hitting a ball

○ giving a hug

○ kicking a ball

---

5. To which one might you be <u>devoted</u>?

   ○ bicycles

   ○ friends

   ○ pencils

_____

6. Which one shows that you are a <u>sensitive</u> person?

   ○ You care about other people's feelings.

   ○ You refuse to talk to a classmate.

   ○ You laugh when another person is crying.

TOTAL SCORE: _____ /6

Name _____

Grammar: Describing Words: How Many

▶ **Fill in the circle next to the word that tells how many.**

1. Ten people are on the team.

   ○ team

   ○ Ten

   ○ people

2. Brett can juggle six balls.

   ○ balls

   ○ six

   ○ juggle

3. The farmer has four chicks.

   ○ four

   ○ farmer

   ○ chicks

4. Pam left seven books on her desk.

   ○ Pam

   ○ seven

   ○ books

Grammar: Describing Words: How Many   224

TOTAL SCORE: _____ /4

Oral Reading Fluency

Kent plays games with his Uncle Arthur on weekends. He and Uncle Arthur play tennis, baseball, and cards. They play catch in the backyard. Kent and Uncle Arthur never cheat, and they never keep score. They never care who wins. They just play for fun. They take turns picking games.

One day, Uncle Arthur gave Kent a gift. It was a chess set. Kent asked Uncle Arthur to teach him to play. Kent was eager to play. They played chess on the porch.

Kent had fun playing chess. Uncle Arthur whispered hints to Kent. The hints helped Kent to win when Kent got stuck.

After Kent won his first game, he giggled with glee. "Hurray! Thanks, Uncle Arthur. This is the best gift!"

**Weekly
Lesson Test**
· · · · · · · ·
Lesson 22

Selection Comprehension

▶ **Fill in the circle next to the correct answer.**

I. The animals go up and down the hill to find

○ some more apples.

○ a better place.

○ a new basket.

_____

2. How do you know the animals feel happy?

○ They sing a song.

○ They carry a basket.

○ They walk up and down.

_____

3. What surprises the animals when they go home?

○ The apples are not sweet.

○ The path is very short.

○ The food is gone.

_____

4. "We're Going on a Picnic" could never happen because

○ animals do not eat.

○ animals do not speak.

○ animals do not walk up hills.

▶ **Write an answer to the question.**

5. Who takes the animals' picnic food?

_____

- -

_____

- -

_____

- -

_____

- -

_____

- -

_____

Name _____

Phonics/Spelling: Long vowel /ī/i-e

▶ **Fill in the circle under the word that names each picture.**

1.

    bake   bike   bank
    ○   ○   ○

2.

    line   lane   life
    ○   ○   ○

3.

9

    near   name   nine
    ○   ○   ○

4.

    shirt   shine   shift
    ○   ○   ○

TOTAL SCORE: _____ /4

Phonics/Spelling: Inflections -*ed*, -*ing*

▶ **Read the sentence. Fill in the circle next to the word that correctly completes the sentence.**

I. Tomas likes _____ his new bike.

○ ridding

○ rideing

○ riding

2. Sam went _____ this weekend.

○ hiking

○ hikeing

○ hikking

3. My shoes are _____ in the corner.

○ pilled

○ piled

○ pileed

4. Mr. Smith _____ to us.

○ wavved

○ waveed

○ waved

TOTAL SCORE: _____ /4

Name _____

High-Frequency Words

▶ **Write a word from the box to complete each sentence.**

┌───┐
│ because   light   right   those   walked   │
└───┘

1. We saw the _____ way to play
the game.

_____

2. The sun will _____ the sky.

_____

3. The girls went in _____ it started
to rain.

_____

4. Pam and Beth did not ride the bus today. They

_____

- -

_____ .

_____

_____

- -

5. _____ apples are ripe.

Name _____

Focus Skill: Problem/Solution

▶ **Read along as your teacher reads each problem. Then circle the better solution.**

1. **Ellen plays at Jane's house. Jane wants to have a tea party with her dolls. Ellen wants to play with her bears. Fill in the answer circle under the picture that shows the solution to the girls' problem.**

      ○   ○

2. **Chase and Josh walk to class. Josh has a backpack. Chase does not. Chase has too many books. What should Chase do? Fill in the answer circle under the picture that shows the solution to Chase's problem.**

      ○   ○

Focus Skill: Problem/Solution

3. Gail looks for a book to read. She wants to read a book about anteaters. She cannot find one. What should Gail do? Fill in the answer circle under the picture that shows the solution to Gail's problem.

    ◯   ◯

---

4. Jack likes his little sister, but she fusses and cries. Jack does not like to hear her cry. What should Jack do? Fill in the answer circle under the picture that shows the solution to Jack's problem.

    ◯   ◯

Focus Skill: Problem/Solution

TOTAL SCORE: _____ /4

Name _____

Robust Vocabulary

▶ **Fill in the circle next to the correct answer.**

1. Which one would you call an <u>incident</u>?

   ○ falling on ice

   ○ sleeping in bed

   ○ reading a book

2. Which one of these would happen in a <u>gradual</u> way?

   ○ ice melting

   ○ rain falling

   ○ a clock ticking

3. Which one would you find helpful in a
   <u>downpour</u>?

   ○ a raincoat

   ○ a hamster

   ○ a candle

4. Which one might you <u>seek</u> after school?

○ a tree

○ a duck

○ a snack

---

5. If someone calls you <u>indecisive</u>, what should you do?

○ make up your mind

○ write a story

○ sew on a button

---

6. Which one might happen if you are <u>oblivious</u> to the rain?

○ You might get wet.

○ You might eat lunch early.

○ You might go swimming.

TOTAL SCORE: _____ /6

Name _____

Grammar: Describing Words: Feelings

▶ **Fill in the circle next to the word that describes feelings.**

1. Rob felt sad when his team lost.

○ sad

○ team

○ lost

2. The boy smiled when he was happy.

○ boy

○ smiled

○ happy

3. Beth was surprised to see her uncle.

○ Beth

○ surprised

○ visit

4. Fran felt hungry before lunch.

○ hungry

○ Fran

○ lunch

Grammar: Describing Words: Feelings   236   TOTAL SCORE: _____ /4

Oral Reading Fluency

Todd and Chad went to the seashore with Mom and Dad on Sunday. Todd played in the sand on the beach. Todd had a bucket. He filled it with sand. Chad played in the mud on the shore. He saw a starfish. Mom and Dad sat in the sun reading.

For lunch, they ate sandwiches. Chad had an apple. Todd had grapes.

After lunch, they sailed on a yellow sailboat. Todd helped his mom steer the boat.

Chad asked to go fishing. He wanted to catch one of the big fish he saw in the clear waves. Dad helped him. Chad had fun on the boat. He grinned at his dad.

At sunset, they went back to the shore. Todd and Chad had fun at the beach.

Selection Comprehension

▶ **Fill in the circle next to the correct answer.**

1. What is this story about?

   ○ a ball game in a park

   ○ things that happen one day

   ○ songs about people and places

---

2. What do Jack and his mother help Mr. Jones do?

   ○ sing songs

   ○ walk the dog

   ○ sweep the leaves

---

3. What does Jack hope to get one day?

   ○ a dog

   ○ a bike

   ○ a big truck

---

4. How does Jack feel about the place where he lives?

   ○ He loves it.

   ○ He is sad about it.

   ○ He is puzzled by it.

▶ **Write an answer to the question.**

5. What is one thing Jack might do the next time it is a pretty day?

_____

- -

_____

- -

_____

- -

_____

- -

_____

- -

_____

Name _____

Phonics/Spelling: Long Vowel /ō/o-e

▶ **Fill in the circle under the word that names each picture.**

1.

rope	rap	ripe
○	○	○

2.

roast	rode	rose
○	○	○

3.

home	hope	hose
○	○	○

4.

stone	store	storm
○	○	○

TOTAL SCORE: _____ /4

Name _____

High-Frequency Words

▶ **Write a word from the box to complete each sentence.**

| brown | city | hello | loudly | love | pulled |

1. The dog has a black coat with

_____

_____ spots.

_____

_____

----

2. Jasper _____ the latch on the

door.

_____

_____

----

3. Neal yelled _____ when the team

scored.

_____

4. Kathleen lives in a

_____
----
big _____ .

_____

_____
----

5. We start the day by saying _____
to Miss Sanchez.

_____

_____
----

6. I _____ my sister Tess.

Focus Skill: Draw Conclusions

▶ **Read the story. Look at the picture. Fill in the circle above the sentence that draws a conclusion about the story.**

1. Seth had a bath. He brushed his teeth. Now he has on a bathrobe. His mom will read him a story.

○   ○

Seth is getting ready for bed.   Seth is going to eat lunch.

---

2. Jade feels hot. Her cheeks are red. Her throat hurts. She does not want to eat.

○   ○

Jade is sick.   Jade feels happy.

Focus Skill: Draw Conclusions

3. Kate's room is painted pink. The lamp beside her bed is pink. She got a pink dress for her birthday.

○

Kate likes to read books.

○

Kate likes the color pink.

4. Kirk sees a small animal. The animal is black with a white stripe. The animal is looking for bugs in Kirk's backyard.

○

The animal is a cow.

○

The animal is a skunk.

5. A breeze rattles the windows. Dennis hears thunder. He feels a drop of rain.

○

A storm is coming soon.

○

The ball game is over.

Focus Skill: Draw Conclusions

244

TOTAL SCORE: _____ /5

Robust Vocabulary

▶ **Fill in the circle next to the correct answer.**

1. If you <u>asserted</u> your opinion, what did you do?

○ You said what you believed in a strong way.

○ You said what another person wanted to hear.

○ You said what your friend told you to say.

2. Which one might make you feel <u>offended</u>?

○ a person who gave you a hug

○ a person who handed you a gift

○ a person who argued with you

3. If you <u>retorted</u> to something someone said, how might your voice sound?

○ sad

○ angry

○ tired

4. Which one is a <u>congenial</u> way to act?

○ ignoring a person who is talking to you

○ opening a door for another person

○ refusing to take out the trash

5. If your teacher tells the class to <u>congregate</u> at the back of the room, what will you do?

○ take off your shoes and socks

○ eat your sandwich slowly

○ walk to the back of the room

6. Which one might you say to be <u>cheerful</u> to another person?

○ "Have a good day!"

○ "What do you want?"

○ "I'm so angry with you!"

Robust Vocabulary

246

TOTAL SCORE: _____ /6

Grammar: Describing Words: -er, -est

▶ **Fill in the circle next to the describing word that compares people.**

1. Tom is taller than Brad.

- ○ Tom
- ○ taller
- ○ Brad

2. Helen is older than Bill.

- ○ older
- ○ Bill
- ○ than

3. Arthur is the bravest of the three men.

- ○ Arthur
- ○ the
- ○ bravest

4. Pam is the shortest girl on the team.

- ○ Pam
- ○ shortest
- ○ team

TOTAL SCORE: _____ /4

Oral Reading Fluency

Elephants are big gray animals. Many elephants live in jungles. Elephants have long trunks. Some have tusks. Elephants use their trunks to help them pick up things. Elephants can pick up branches with their trunks. Elephants use their trunks to eat leaves and to drink water. Tusks help elephants dig and eat.

Elephants have big ears. They flap their ears when they get hot. Elephants have tails. They use their tails to keep insects away.

Elephants are smart. Some elephants can paint. The elephant holds the brush with its trunk. The elephant dips the brush in the paint. Then the elephant makes a pattern on paper with the paint.

Selection Comprehension

▶ **Fill in the circle next to the correct answer.**

1. What do the children want to find out?

○ where someone lives

○ what people do at night

○ who sang the night song

2. How do the children know Mrs. Price has a visitor?

○ Mrs. Lane tells them.

○ Ann sees a black bag.

○ Kate sees someone in the window.

3. What can you tell about the visitor?

○ She likes the night sky.

○ She will visit Mrs. Price again.

○ She is friends with Kate's mother.

4. The visitor turns out to be Mrs. Price's

○ friend.

○ mother.

○ sister.

▶ **Write an answer to the question.**

5. What happens at the end of the story?

_____

- -

_____

- -

_____

- -

_____

- -

_____

- -

_____

Name _____

High-Frequency Words

▶ **Write a word from the box to complete each sentence.**

become	busy	eyes	high
remembered	talk	visitor	listen

1. Ann was too _____ to help her sister.

2. Freckles the cat has green _____ .

3. A frog can jump _____ in the air.

4. Pam and Ellen like to _____ to that song.

5. A tadpole will _____ a frog
one day.

_____

6. A _____ came to art class today.

_____

7. Jack _____ to bring his backpack.
He forgot it last week.

_____

8. Lester likes to _____ to his
pal Stan.

Focus Skill: Draw Conclusions

▶ **Read the story. Look at the picture. Circle
the sentence that draws a conclusion.**

1. Beth feeds the chicks. She checks the latch
on the gate. She leads the sheep to the pen.
She hears the pigs squeal. She feeds them
turnips.

○   ○

Beth is on a farm.   Beth is at the mall.

---

2. Dean and his dad came to the perfect spot.
They put up the tent. Then Dean's dad made
a fire. They slept in sleeping bags.

○   ○

Dean and his Dad are   Dean and his Dad
at a shop.   are camping.

Focus Skill: Draw Conclusions

3. The sun was a big yellow ball. The air
coming into the van was hot. Blake saw
a snake slither in the sand. It rested under
a cactus. Blake had not felt this hot before.

○   ○

Blake was in the desert.   Blake likes snakes.

---

4. Gwen kicked the ball. The team ran beside her.
She kicked the black and white ball again. It
went into the net. Her mom and dad cheered.

○   ○

Gwen scored a goal.   Gwen cannot run fast.

Name _____

Robust Vocabulary

▶ **Fill in the circle next to the correct answer.**

1. With which one might you be <u>pleased</u>?

   ○ walking to school

   ○ eating a lemon

   ○ doing well on a test

2. Which one might give you <u>joy</u>?

   ○ an unexpected gift

   ○ a sneaker with holes

   ○ a bag of smelly trash

3. When might you have <u>stammered</u>?

   ○ cheering your team

   ○ talking in front of many people

   ○ whispering to a friend

4. Which one is <u>puzzling</u>?

○ a dog that talks

○ the moon at night

○ a school bell that rings

_____

5. In which job would a person be <u>probing</u> for answers?

○ chef

○ scientist

○ mover

_____

6. If you are <u>unrelenting</u>, what are you doing?

○ You are acting funny.

○ You are going to sleep.

○ You keep trying.

TOTAL SCORE: _____ /6

Grammar: Troublesome Words: Multiple-Meaning Words

▶ **Fill in the circle next to the meaning of the underlined word.**

1. A <u>bat</u> lives in the attic.

○ a small animal that flies

○ a stick made of wood

2. Josh and Tina <u>shine</u> their shoes.

○ to make brighter

○ to give light

3. Mom gave me a dollar <u>bill</u>.

○ the hard mouth part of a duck

○ a piece of paper money

4. There are many flowers in the <u>spring</u>.

○ to jump up quickly

○ season of the year

Oral Reading Fluency

Gwen likes playing in the park near her house. She meets playmates at the park gates. The children take turns swinging on the swing set. Gwen likes swinging.

Gwen's mom sits on a park bench near the path. She smiles at Gwen.

The children play tag and leapfrog. Gwen likes running fast.

The children have a picnic. Gwen has a sandwich and popcorn.

Then Gwen's mom blows bubbles. The wind blows the bubbles away. Gwen chases the bubbles.

Ducks swim in the pond in the park. Gwen feeds the ducks. The ducks quack and eat.

In the tall trees, birds chirp and sing.

Squirrels hide nuts in the tree branches. Rabbits hop near the path and hide in the shrubs.

Gwen and her mom have fun at the park.

Name _____

Selection Comprehension

▶ **Fill in the circle next to the correct answer.**

1. What is this story about?

○ A turtle has a shell that is very hard.

○ Ducks use their webbed feet as paddles.

○ Animals have many things that help them to live.

---

2. What helps animals to hide?

○ spots and color

○ quills and humps

○ long necks and noses

---

3. Tail flukes and webbed feet are the SAME because

○ they both stay clean.

○ they help animals to swim fast.

○ animals need them to reach food.

---

4. The writer wants to

○ make you smile.

○ teach about some animals.

○ show how to color a turtle shell.

Name _____

▶ **Write an answer to the question.**

5. What is another animal that has fur to keep it warm?

_____

- -

_____

- -

_____

- -

_____

- -

_____

- -

_____

- -

Selection Comprehension
"Amazing Animals"

TOTAL SCORE: _____ /4 + _____ /2

Name _____

Phonics/Spelling: Long Vowel /(y)o͞o/ *u-e*

▶ **Fill in the circle under the word that names each picture.**

1.

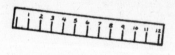

ruler   rude   robe

○   ○   ○

2.

turn   tube   tune

○   ○   ○

3.

cute   curb   cube

○   ○   ○

4.

mule   mile   male

○   ○   ○

TOTAL SCORE: _____ /4

High-Frequency Words

▶ **Write a word from the box to complete each sentence.**

```
clear  color  good-bye  hair  kinds  only  toes
```

_____
----

1. Brad has _____ one sister.

_____

_____
----

2. Dad will say _____ before he leaves.

_____

_____
----

3. It was _____ after the storm.

_____

4. Dan likes eating all _____ of ice
cream.

_____

5. Kate brushed her _____.

_____

6. Jess likes the _____ yellow best.

_____

7. Can you wiggle your _____?

Focus Skill: Alphabetize

▶ **Fill in the circle next to the group of words that are in ABC order.**

1. | cat   sat   bat   rat |

○ sat, bat, cat, rat

○ bat, cat, rat, sat

○ rat, sat, bat, cat

2. | ant   picnic   hide   napkin |

○ ant, napkin, hide, picnic

○ hide, picnic, ant, napkin

○ ant, hide, napkin, picnic

3. | sand   bird   tree   float |

○ bird, float, sand, tree

○ tree, sand, float, bird

○ float, bird, sand, tree

Focus Skill: Alphabetize

TOTAL SCORE: _____ /3

Robust Vocabulary

▶ **Fill in the circle next to the correct answer.**

1. Which one do you think is <u>incredible</u>?

○ an astronaut going to the moon

○ a dog that barks at strangers

○ a glass of water from a faucet

2. What do you do on a <u>typical</u> morning?

○ You say goodnight.

○ You sing along with your dog.

○ You eat breakfast.

3. Which one has great <u>variety</u>?

○ a single rose

○ a rose bush

○ a flower shop

4. Which one is a <u>peaceful</u> place to be?

○ a soccer game

○ a funny movie

○ a garden

5. Which one does a pet <u>deserve</u> for doing
a trick?

○ a long bath

○ a treat

○ angry words

---

6. Which one is something that you <u>usually</u> do
after school?

○ have a snack

○ watch a parade

○ receive a gift

Name _____

Grammar Skill: Verbs

▶ **Fill in the circle next to the word that describes an action in each sentence.**

1. Nate marched in the band last summer.

- ○ Nate
- ○ marched
- ○ summer

2. Blake leaped up into the air.

- ○ leaped
- ○ up
- ○ Blake

3. Bess ran to the top of the hill.

- ○ Bess
- ○ ran
- ○ top

4. Ten fish swam in the pond.

- ○ Ten
- ○ fish
- ○ swam

Grammar Skill: Verbs   267   TOTAL SCORE: _____ /4

Oral Reading Fluency

Blake wishes for a pet. He likes dogs. He asks his dad for a pup.

Blake's dad says that he can have a pup.

Blake's pup is small and black. He has a long tail and short ears. Blake calls his pup Bubbles.

He gives Bubbles food and water.

Blake puts Bubbles in the bathtub for a bath. Bubbles splashes in the suds. He likes the water.

Then Blake brushes Bubbles coat. Bubbles' fur is soft.

In the backyard, Blake plays with Bubbles. Bubbles runs after the ball. He brings the ball to Blake. Blake gives Bubbles treats. Bubbles likes treats.

Blake and his dad take Bubbles to the park on a leash. Bubbles barks at the other animals.

Blake loves his pup.

Name _____

Selection Comprehension

▶ **Fill in the circle next to the correct answer.**

1. Little Bear thinks he can do what birds do because

   ○ wings will help him fly.

   ○ birds have a little plane.

   ○ he has a new helmet.

2. What happens when Little Bear jumps from the tree?

   ○ He flies high in the sky.

   ○ He tumbles down a hill.

   ○ He lands on a star far away.

3. Where is Little Bear at the end?

   ○ up in a tree

   ○ high in the sky

   ○ in his own house

4. Which word BEST tells about Little Bear?

   ○ dreamer

   ○ worker

   ○ writer

Name _____

▶ **Write an answer to the question.**

5. What does Little Bear do at the end of the story?

_____

- -

_____

- -

_____

- -

_____

- -

_____

- -

_____

Selection Comprehension
"Little Bear Goes to the Moon"

270

TOTAL SCORE: _____ /4 + _____ /2

© Harcourt • Grade 1

Phonics/Spelling: Long Vowel

▶ **Fill in the circle under the word that names
each picture.**

1.

pie	pinch	pile
○	○	○

2.

sly	skid	sky
○	○	○

3.

tries	tire	ties
○	○	○

4.

night	nice	nine
○	○	○

TOTAL SCORE: _____ /4

Name _____

Phonics/Spelling: Contraction 'd

▶ **Fill in the circle next to the words that make up the underlined contraction.**

1. Who'd like to come with me?

   ○ Who did

   ○ Who would

   ○ Who is

2. We'd like to leave early.

   ○ We did

   ○ We don't

   ○ We would

3. You'd better read this book.

   ○ You had

   ○ You would

   ○ You could

4. They'd like to play in the park.

   ○ They had

   ○ They would

   ○ They could

Phonics/Spelling: Contraction 'd   272   TOTAL SCORE: _____ /4

High-Frequency Words

▶ **Write a word from the box to complete each sentence.**

| climbed   earth   fooling   thought   table |

1. I _____ the room was too hot.

2. The bird flew high in the sky then back to

_____ .

3. The children are just _____

around.

© Harcourt • Grade 1

_____

4. Janet _____ the stairs to her
room.

_____

5. Please get your backpack off the

_____

- -

_____ .

Focus Skill: Story Elements

▶ **Read the story. Then fill in the circle next to the correct answer.**

Franklin likes to go to the beach with his mom and his sister Gail. He likes to look at the waves. The sun is hot and a wind blows on his face. He likes the way the sand feels on his feet. Gail digs in the sand and puts it into a bucket. Mom brings a picnic lunch for them to eat.

A big wave comes up on the shore. It gets the children's feet wet. The wave goes back out into the sea. Now there are small shells by Franklin's feet. The shells are very pretty. One shell is white and pink. Franklin picks it up to take home.

Focus Skill: Story Elements

© Harcourt • Grade 1

I. Who is this story about?

○ sand and waves

○ Franklin, Gail, and their mom

○ small, pretty shells

---

2. Where does this story happen?

○ at the beach

○ at a school

○ in a house

---

3. What is it about?

○ a family's day at the beach

○ the colors of shells

○ sand and how it feels

Name _____

Robust Vocabulary

▶ **Fill in the circle next to the correct answer.**

1. If you have a <u>pale</u> blue shirt, what color is it?

   ○ light blue

   ○ dark blue

   ○ bright blue

2. Of which one might you think <u>fondly</u>?

   ○ a cactus

   ○ a pet

   ○ a rock

3. How might you feel in a <u>shadowy</u> room?

   ○ frightened

   ○ bored

   ○ silly

4. If someone is <u>imaginative</u>, they are

○ good at soccer.

○ running in a race.

○ good at coming up with ideas.

5. If you and your friend have <u>similar</u> tastes in books, what do you do?

○ You read different kind of books.

○ You read the same kind of books.

○ You prefer to carry your own books.

6. To which one might you feel <u>affectionate</u>?

○ your bicycle

○ your backpack

○ your family

TOTAL SCORE: _____ /6

Grammar: Verbs That Tell About Now

▶ **Fill in the circle next to the verb that tells about now.**

1. I _____ a nest in the tree.

   ○ see

   ○ seen

   ○ saw

2. The kitten _____ for its mother.

   ○ cried

   ○ carried

   ○ cries

3. Albert _____ the birds in the backyard.

   ○ fed

   ○ food

   ○ feeds

4. The children _____ near the park.

   ○ lived

   ○ live

   ○ lied

TOTAL SCORE: _____ /4

Oral Reading Fluency

Dale went to the circus on Thursday with his mom and dad and little sister Bess. They had so much fun.

First, he saw lots of animals. He liked the elephants best. Then he went into a big tent. He saw men in costumes with red noses and long ties. They drove a very little green car. In the center ring, a man had on a tall black hat and a cape. He did magic tricks.

Up in the air, people walked on a rope that had a net under it. A girl did a flip on the rope.

There were so many things to see.

Mom and dad got snacks for Dale and Bess.

Dale and Bess want to go to the circus again.

_____ /WCPM

Name _____

Selection Comprehension

▶ **Fill in the circle next to the correct answer.**

1. What is Ebb doing at the BEGINNING?

○ playing in the sand

○ listening to the rain

○ talking to the ducks

2. Where do Ebb and a baby seal spend the day?

○ at the beach

○ in a house

○ on a boat

3. What does the baby seal need?

○ a friend

○ some food

○ its mother

4. Where does Mom take the baby seal?

○ to a pet store

○ to its home

○ to a zoo

Name _____

▶ **Write an answer to the question.**

5. What will Ebb and the baby seal do the next time they are together?

_____
- -
_____
- -
_____
- -
_____
- -
_____
- -
_____
- -
_____
- -
_____

High-Frequency Words

▶ **Write a word from the box to complete each sentence.**

answered	baby	done	heard
pools	pushed	together	

1. Bart and Jim play ball _____.

2. I _____ by nodding my head.

3. Stan held his _____ sister Beth.

4. The ducks played in the _____ of water.

5. Jess said that she was

_____

_____ eating her lunch.

6. Chad and Mack _____ the crow.

7. Jay _____ his sister on the swing.

Focus Skill: Story Elements

▶ **Read the story. Then fill in the circle next to the correct answer.**

Meg likes to do cartwheels. She does cartwheels for friends. She does cartwheels for pets. She does cartwheels for people she has never met!

When Meg wakes up, she hops out of bed. She does a cartwheel out of her room. She does a cartwheel when she sees Mom and Dad. Mom looks at Dad. Dad looks at Mom. They shake their heads.

Meg jumps to the school bus. Mr. Miller drives the bus. He shakes his head.

Meg likes to do cartwheels at school. Children in her class look at Meg. They shake their heads.

"We are going to do something fun," the teacher says. "Meg can help us. She is going to teach us to do cartwheels."

The teacher smiles at Meg. "What can I do but shake my head?" asks the teacher.

1. Who is this story about?

○ Mom and Dad

○ Meg

○ Mr. Miller

_____

2. Where does this story happen?

○ at Meg's house and school

○ in a forest

○ at the zoo

_____

3. What is it about?

○ Meg likes to do cartwheels all the time.

○ Children can ride a bus to school.

○ Teachers can do cartwheels.

Focus Skill: Story Elements

286

TOTAL SCORE: _____ /3

Robust Vocabulary

▶ **Fill in the circle next to the correct answer.**

I. If you <u>quivered</u> because of the weather, how did you feel?

○ wet

○ warm

○ cold

2. If you <u>wailed</u> at the sight of a spider, what did you do?

○ You let out a loud cry.

○ You whispered to a friend.

○ You jumped back in fear.

3. If friends <u>scattered</u> in the mall, what did they do?

○ They walked together to a store.

○ They went in different directions.

○ They ran to the food court.

Name _____

4. What might be a good thing to do if you are lonesome?

○ play with a friend

○ take a nap

○ spend time by yourself

5. What might you do if you are elated?

○ stomp your feet because you are very upset

○ jump up and down because you are happy and excited

○ sit quietly in a chair because you are tired

6. If it seemed hopeless to find something you lost, how would you feel?

○ ready to take a nap

○ happy it was gone

○ there was no chance to find it

Grammar: Using *Am*, *Is*, and *Are*

▶ **Fill in the circle next to the word that best completes each sentence.**

I. Brett and Ann _____ friends.

 ○ am

 ○ are

 ○ is

2. It _____ my bedtime.

 ○ am

 ○ are

 ○ is

3. I _____ glad to see you.

 ○ am

 ○ are

 ○ is

4. Our class _____ going to the park.

 ○ am

 ○ are

 ○ is

TOTAL SCORE: _____ /4

Oral Reading Fluency

Pythons are a type of snake. Pythons can be tan with brown spots. They have scales. They do not have lids over their eyes. Pythons can be big or small. Pythons grow every year that they live.

Pythons are long and thin and have no arms or legs. They slither on the ground and in trees. They smell and see well. This helps them hunt.

Pythons hunt for their food. Pythons eat birds, frogs, and small animals.

Pythons can live under the ground or in trees. Pythons can live near or in rivers and lakes. Pythons can swim.

Pythons lay eggs and like to lie on rocks in the sun.

Selection Comprehension

▶ **Fill in the circle next to the correct answer.**

1. What is the story about?

   ○ how crayons are made

   ○ who gave crayons their name

   ○ when people first used crayons

2. A crayon starts out as

   ○ powder.

   ○ water.

   ○ wax.

3. How are crayons the SAME?

   ○ All are one color.

   ○ All get packed in boxes.

   ○ All have the same color name.

4. What part of the story could never happen?

   ○ putting a crayon on a shelf

   ○ using a crayon to color

   ○ a crayon talking

▶ **Write an answer to the question.**

5. What is one thing Kelly will color with her red crayon?

_____

_____

_____

_____

_____

_____

Name _____

High-Frequency Words

▶ **Write a word from the box to complete each sentence.**

| blue   great   poured   traveled   able   took   almost |

1. I made a red and _____ kite.

2. My family _____ on a bus.

3. Sal _____ the milk for us.

4. Nate was _____ to find his backpack.

_____
----

5. Vicky _____ the book from the table.

_____

_____
----

6. Jake _____ hit the ball.

_____

_____
----

7. This story is about a _____ white whale.

Focus Skill: Details

▶ **Read the story. Then fill in the circle next to the correct answer.**

Cow, Pig, and Sheep all live on Jay's farm. A goat named Gwen and a hen named Jen lived on Jay's farm, too.

Cow, Pig, and Sheep got along well. Gwen the Goat liked to start trouble. Every day, Jay gave Jen the Hen her corn. Then he went to feed Cow, Pig, and Sheep. Gwen got her corn last.

Gwen did not like eating last. One day Gwen jumped out of her pen. She hid near Jen. Jay gave Jen her corn. Then Jay went to feed Cow. Gwen came from her hiding place and started to eat Jen's corn!

Jay ran back to Jen's pen. "Gwen! That corn is Jen's! Go back to your pen."

Gwen was sad. She wished that she had been a good goat. "Gwen," said Jay. "Behave and I'll feed you first this weekend."

Gwen was happy. She got into her pen. Now Gwen would be a very good goat!

I. What is the setting of this story?

○ a street

○ a farm

○ a park

_____

2. Which animals get along well?

○ Gwen and Jen

○ Cow, Pig, and Sheep

○ Pig and Gwen

_____

3. Who starts to eat Jen's corn?

○ Gwen

○ Cow

○ Jay

_____

4. Why is Gwen happy at the end of the story?

○ Cow, Pig, and Sheep like Gwen.

○ Jen gave her corn to Gwen.

○ Jay will feed her first on the weekend.

Focus Skill: Details

TOTAL SCORE: _____ /4

Teacher Read-Aloud

Name _____

Weekly
Lesson Test
. . . .
Lesson 28

Robust Vocabulary

▶ **Fill in the circle next to the correct answer.**

1. How do you feel when you see a <u>familiar</u> face?

○ bored

○ sad

○ happy

_____

2. What do you say to a person who has <u>arrived</u>
at your house?

○ "Thank you."

○ "Hello."

○ "Good-bye,"

_____

3. Which one is an example of acting <u>properly</u>?

○ saying "please" and "thank you"

○ talking with your mouth full

○ taking someone else's lunch

_____

4. Which one might you <u>anticipate</u>?

○ a visit to the doctor

○ a party with your family

○ a trip to empty the trash

---

5. If you have <u>numerous</u> pennies, how many might you have?

○ one

○ thirteen

○ none

---

6. If you use <u>vibrant</u> paints, how will your painting look?

○ plain

○ dull

○ bright

Grammar: Verbs That Tell About the Past

▶ **Fill in the circle next to the verb that tells about the past.**

1. Yesterday, I _____ a cake with my sister.

   ○ baking

   ○ bake

   ○ baked

2. Jimmy _____ into the lamp and it fell.

   ○ bump

   ○ bumped

   ○ bumps

3. Annie _____ the spelling test.

   ○ passed

   ○ passing

   ○ pass

4. Last night, our dog Freckles _____ a cat!

   ○ chases

   ○ chased

   ○ chase

TOTAL SCORE: _____ /4

Oral Reading Fluency

Ellen and Greg had fun blowing soap bubbles. Ellen held a stick with a circle on the end. She had a bottle of soap, too. "I'll blow three bubbles," she said. She dipped the stick into the bottle. She blew three big bubbles. They floated over her head.

"I'll blow five bubbles," said Greg. He blew in the circle. Five bubbles floated in the air. Ellen and Greg kept blowing bubbles. Soon bubbles were all over!

Ellen put her finger on a bubble. It popped and soap got on her. She grinned and popped more bubbles. The bubbles got soap on Greg.

Then Greg popped bubbles on Ellen. Soon, they were soapy and wet. Ellen and Greg were as soapy as the bubbles!

Name _____

Selection Comprehension

▶ **Fill in the circle next to the correct answer.**

1. What happens FIRST?

○ A girl rakes a road.

○ Jen digs in the sand.

○ A boy makes a moat.

---

2. Why does a girl dig a path to the lake?

○ to make the moat look pretty

○ to help people reach the moat

○ to fill the moat with water

---

3. How are the beach friends the SAME?

○ All build a wall.

○ All make a road.

○ All play in the sand.

---

4. Why do the friends kick down their sand castle?

○ They think it is too small.

○ They don't want others to see it.

○ They know they can build again.

Name _____

▶ **Write an answer to the question.**

5. What will the beach friends do tomorrow?

_____

_____

_____

_____

_____

_____

High-Frequency Words

▶ **Write a word from the box to complete
each sentence.**

| boy | building | tomorrow | toward | welcoming |

1. Brent is a _____ in my class.

_____

2. Seeing her mom's _____ smile, the baby
stopped crying.

_____

3. The children ran _____ the net.

_____
- -

4. My little brother is _____ a bridge
with blocks.

_____

5. Miss Smith's class will read a silly story

_____
- -
_____ .

Focus Skill: Details

▶ **Read the story. Then fill in the circle next to the correct answer.**

Thursday is the class costume party! We are dressing as farm animals. I am going to be a cow. My name is Molly. So, I will be Molly the Cow.

My mom and I made my cow costume. We got a white sheet. I painted big black spots on it, just like a real cow. We made a pink nose. We made ears from paper cups. The ears are fun!

My costume has a long tail. I tied a string to it. When I pull the string, the tail swings.

I have black socks on my hands and feet. They look like cow's feet.

I think my cow costume will be a hit. I think I will be the best cow in class!

I. Where is the costume party?

○ in a house

○ in class

○ in a park

---

2. Who helps Molly make her costume?

○ her friends

○ her mom

○ her teacher

---

3. What color is the costume's nose?

○ pink

○ white

○ black

---

4. How does the tail move?

○ Molly paints on spots.

○ Molly puts on mittens.

○ Molly pulls a string.

Focus Skill: Details

TOTAL SCORE: _____ /4

Robust Vocabulary

▶ **Fill in the circle next to the correct answer.**

1. If you touched a <u>prickly</u> plant, how might it feel?

   ○ sharp

   ○ bumpy

   ○ smooth

2. If you are <u>interested</u> in music, what might you do?

   ○ become bored at concerts

   ○ stop listening to the radio

   ○ learn to play an instrument

3. Which might you do if you are <u>cooperative</u>?

   ○ argue with friends

   ○ work together with classmates

   ○ refuse to help with chores

4. If you <u>construct</u> a model car, what do you do?

○ break it

○ throw it away

○ build it

5. If you <u>assist</u> someone who is making a sand castle, what do you do?

○ help build it

○ walk around it

○ pour water on it

6. If you see a worm <u>wriggle</u>, what is it doing?

○ taking a nap

○ moving back and forth

○ staying very still

Name _____

Grammar: Using *Was* and *Were*

► **Fill in the circle next to the word that completes each sentence.**

1. We _____ playing a game of checkers.

   ○ were

   ○ was

_____

2. Where _____ your sister?

   ○ were

   ○ was

_____

3. Andy _____ the only person I played with.

   ○ were

   ○ was

_____

4. The puppies _____ barking all day.

   ○ were

   ○ was

Grammar: Using *Was* and *Were*

TOTAL SCORE: _____ /4

Oral Reading Fluency

Frank wants to have a party at noon on Sunday. He will have it in his backyard. He hopes it will not rain. He asks five friends. Kate, Jack, Bob, and Tess say they can make it to Frank's party. Jen cannot come.

First, Frank must get food. He wants to have tacos. His dad helps Frank make the tacos.

Then Frank sets up a table in the backyard. His mom puts a yellow cloth on the table.

Frank picks the games he and his friends will play. He thinks his friends will have fun playing soccer. He gets his soccer ball out.

As his friends come, Frank is happy. The sun is out. He thinks his party will be fun!

Name _____

Selection Comprehension

▶ **Fill in the circle next to the correct answer.**

1. Why does Toad make a list?

○ to make him feel grand

○ to help him remember

○ to show off to friends

2. How does Toad feel when his list blows away?

○ upset

○ lucky

○ proud

3. What happens LAST?

○ Toad wakes up.

○ Toad walks with Frog.

○ Toad and Frog go to sleep.

4. Why could this story never happen?

○ Toads do not eat.

○ Toads do not sleep.

○ Toads do not make lists.

Name _____

Lesson 30

▶ **Write an answer to the question.**

5. What part of the story did you like the BEST?

_____
- -
_____
- -
_____
- -
_____
- -
_____
- -
_____
- -
_____
- -
_____
- -
_____
- -

Selection Comprehension
"Frog and Toad Together"

312

TOTAL SCORE: _____ /4 + _____ /2

© Harcourt • Grade 1

High-Frequency Words

▶ **Write a word from the box to complete each sentence.**

| ready | sorry | front | any | nothing |

_____

1. Ann does not have _____ milk.

_____

2. The backpack has _____ in it.

_____

3. Bert has his backpack and is _____ to go to school.

4. I'm _____ that I forgot your birthday.

_____

5. Ellen came in the _____ door.

Focus Skill: Alphabetize

▶ **Put the words in ABC order.**

1.
| horn   bump   seat   gift |

- ○ seat, bump, gift, horn
- ○ bump, gift, horn, seat
- ○ gift, horn, seat, bump

2.
| toss   clap   magnet   sit |

- ○ clap, magnet, sit, toss
- ○ magnet, toss, sit, clap
- ○ sit, clap, toss, magnet

3.
| wave   dent   rug   marble |

- ○ marble, wave, dent, rug
- ○ rug, wave, marble, dent
- ○ dent, marble, rug, wave

TOTAL SCORE: _____ /3

Name _____

Robust Vocabulary

▶ **Fill in the circle next to the correct answer.**

1. What is a <u>tremendous</u> noise you might hear?

   ○ someone humming a song softly

   ○ a loud crash

   ○ a friend speaking in a quiet voice

2. If you <u>seized</u> a football, what did you do?

   ○ bounced it

   ○ dropped it

   ○ grabbed it

3. After which one might you feel <u>exhausted</u>?

   ○ running a race

   ○ taking a nap

   ○ watching a movie.

Robust Vocabulary

4. When might you have a hard time being patient?

○ when you are reading an interesting book

○ when you want to open a gift

○ when you are eating dinner with family

5. Which one might you find tiresome?

○ walking a long way

○ playing video games

○ skating in the park

6. Which one might be outrageous?

○ throwing a stick to a dog

○ sweeping the floor with a broom

○ playing piano with your toes

Name _____

Grammar: Using *Go* and *Went*

▶ **Fill in the circle next to the word that completes each sentence.**

I. I will _____ to the park today.

○ went

○ go

_____

2. We _____ to a movie yesterday.

○ went

○ go

_____

3. The men will _____ back to the house.

○ went

○ go

_____

4. We had fun when we _____ to the beach.

○ went

○ go

TOTAL SCORE: _____ /4

Oral Reading Fluency

Lots of animals live in zoos. Children can go on a field trip to a zoo with their teacher.

At the zoo, children can see elephants. Elephants are big and gray and have long trunks. Some elephants have tusks. Elephants are very big animals. The children can go to see the giraffes. Giraffes are yellow and brown. Giraffes have very long necks. Giraffes eat leaves from tall trees.

The children can go to see the snakes. They live in a dark house. Some snakes are long. Some snakes are short. All of the snakes have scales.

The children can go see the penguins swim. The penguins are black and white. The penguins dive in the water. The water is cold. Penguins like cold water.

_____ /WCPM